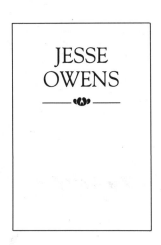

JESSE
OWENS

JESSE OWENS

◆

Tony Gentry

Senior Consulting Editor
Nathan Irvin Huggins
Director
W.E.B. Du Bois Institute for Afro-American Research
Harvard University

CHELSEA HOUSE PUBLISHERS
New York   Philadelphia

CHELSEA HOUSE PUBLISHERS
Editor-in-Chief   Nancy Toff
Executive Editor   Remmel T. Nunn
Managing Editor   Karyn Gullen Browne
Picture Editor   Adrian G. Allen
Art Director   Maria Epes
Manufacturing Manager   Gerald Levine

Black Americans of Achievement
Senior Editor   Richard Rennert

Staff for JESSE OWENS
Deputy Copy Chief   Nicole Bowen
Editorial Assistant   Navorn Johnson
Picture Researcher   Patricia Burns
Assistant Art Director   Loraine Machlin
Designer   James Baker
Production Manager   Joseph Romano
Production Coordinator   Marie Claire Cebrián
Cover Illustration   Alan Nahigian

3   5   7   9   8   6   4   2

Library of Congress Cataloging-in-Publication Data
Gentry, Tony.
Jesse Owens/Tony Gentry.
    p.   cm.—(Black Americans of achievement)
Includes bibliographical references.
Summary: A biography of the track-and-field star who won gold
medals in the 1936 Summer Olympic Games.
ISBN 1-55546-603-6
      0-7910-0247-0 (pbk.)
1. Owens, Jesse, 1913–1980—Juvenile literature.   2. Track-and-field
athletes—United States—Biography—Juvenile literature. [1. Owens,
Jesse. 1913–1980.   2. Track-and-field athletes.   3. Afro-
Americans—Biography.]   I. Title.   II. Series.
GV697.09G46   1990
796.42′092—dc20   89-22354
[B]   CIP
[92]   AC

CONTENTS

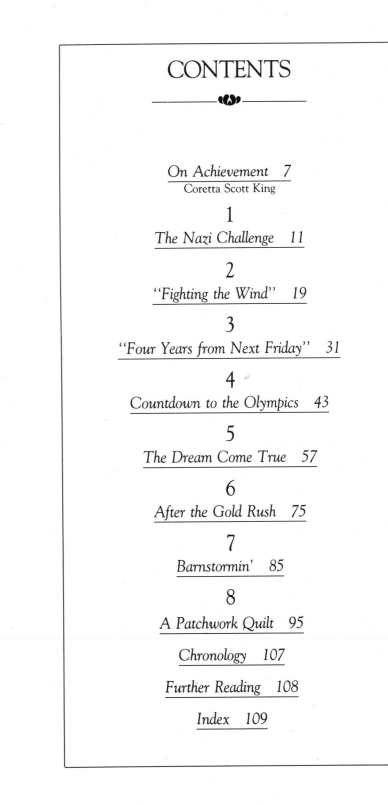

BLACK AMERICANS OF ACHIEVEMENT

RALPH ABERNATHY
civil rights leader

MUHAMMAD ALI
heavyweight champion

RICHARD ALLEN
religious leader and social activist

LOUIS ARMSTRONG
musician

ARTHUR ASHE
tennis great

JOSEPHINE BAKER
entertainer

JAMES BALDWIN
author

BENJAMIN BANNEKER
scientist and mathematician

AMIRI BARAKA
poet and playwright

COUNT BASIE
bandleader and composer

ROMARE BEARDEN
artist

JAMES BECKWOURTH
frontiersman

MARY McLEOD
BETHUNE
educator

BLANCHE BRUCE
politician

RALPH BUNCHE
diplomat

GEORGE WASHINGTON
CARVER
botanist

CHARLES CHESNUTT
author

BILL COSBY
entertainer

PAUL CUFFE
merchant and abolitionist

FATHER DIVINE
religious leader

FREDERICK DOUGLASS
abolitionist editor

CHARLES DREW
physician

W.E.B. DU BOIS
scholar and activist

PAUL LAURENCE DUNBAR
poet

KATHERINE DUNHAM
dancer and choreographer

MARIAN WRIGHT EDELMAN
civil rights leader and lawyer

DUKE ELLINGTON
bandleader and composer

RALPH ELLISON
author

JULIUS ERVING
basketball great

JAMES FARMER
civil rights leader

ELLA FITZGERALD
singer

MARCUS GARVEY
black-nationalist leader

DIZZY GILLESPIE
musician

PRINCE HALL
social reformer

W. C. HANDY
father of the blues

WILLIAM HASTIE
educator and politician

MATTHEW HENSON
explorer

CHESTER HIMES
author

BILLIE HOLIDAY
singer

JOHN HOPE
educator

LENA HORNE
entertainer

LANGSTON HUGHES
poet

ZORA NEALE HURSTON
author

JESSE JACKSON
civil rights leader and politician

JACK JOHNSON
heavyweight champion

JAMES WELDON JOHNSON
author

SCOTT JOPLIN
composer

BARBARA JORDAN
politician

MARTIN LUTHER KING, JR.
civil rights leader

ALAIN LOCKE
scholar and educator

JOE LOUIS
heavyweight champion

RONALD McNAIR
astronaut

MALCOLM X
militant black leader

THURGOOD MARSHALL
Supreme Court justice

ELIJAH MUHAMMAD
religious leader

JESSE OWENS
champion athlete

CHARLIE PARKER
musician

GORDON PARKS
photographer

SIDNEY POITIER
actor

ADAM CLAYTON POWELL, JR.
political leader

LEONTYNE PRICE
opera singer

A. PHILIP RANDOLPH
labor leader

PAUL ROBESON
singer and actor

JACKIE ROBINSON
baseball great

BILL RUSSELL
basketball great

JOHN RUSSWURM
publisher

SOJOURNER TRUTH
antislavery activist

HARRIET TUBMAN
antislavery activist

NAT TURNER
slave revolt leader

DENMARK VESEY
slave revolt leader

MADAME C. J. WALKER
entrepreneur

BOOKER T. WASHINGTON
educator

HAROLD WASHINGTON
politician

WALTER WHITE
civil rights leader and author

RICHARD WRIGHT
author

ON
ACHIEVEMENT

———— ❧ ————

Coretta Scott King

Before you begin this book, I hope you will ask yourself what the word *excellence* means to you. I think that it's a question we should all ask and keep asking as we grow older and change. Because the truest answer to it should never change. When you think of excellence, perhaps you think of success at work; or of becoming wealthy; or meeting the right person, getting married, and having a good family life.

Those important goals are worth striving for, but there is a better way to look at excellence. As Martin Luther King, Jr., said in one of his last sermons, "I want you to be first in love. I want you to be first in moral excellence. I want you to be first in generosity. If you want to be important, wonderful. If you want to be great, wonderful. But recognize that he who is greatest among you shall be your servant."

My husband, Martin Luther King, Jr., knew that the true meaning of achievement is service. When I met him, in 1952, he was already ordained as a Baptist preacher and was working toward a doctoral degree at Boston University. I was studying at the New England Conservatory and dreamed of accomplishments in music. We married a year later, and after I graduated the following year we moved to Montgomery, Alabama. We didn't know it then, but our notions of achievement were about to undergo a dramatic change.

You may have read or heard about what happened next. What began with the boycott of a local bus line grew into a national movement, and by the time he was assassinated in 1968 my husband had fashioned a black movement powerful enough to shatter forever the practice of racial segregation. What you may not have read about is where he got his method for resisting injustice without compromising his religious beliefs.

He adopted the strategy of nonviolence from a man of a different race, who lived in a distant country, and even practiced a different religion. The man was Mahatma Gandhi, the great leader of India, who devoted his life to serving humanity in the spirit of love and nonviolence. It was in these principles that Martin discovered his method for social reform. More than anything else, those two principles were the key to his achievements.

This book is about black Americans who served society through the excellence of their achievements. It forms a part of the rich history of black men and women in America—a history of stunning accomplishments in every field of human endeavor, from literature and art to science, industry, education, diplomacy, athletics, jurisprudence, even polar exploration.

Not all of the people in this history had the same ideals, but I think you will find something that all of them have in common. Like Martin Luther King, Jr., they all decided to become "drum majors" and serve humanity. In that principle—whether it was expressed in books, inventions, or song—they found something outside themselves to use as a goal and a guide. Something that showed them a way to serve others, instead of living only for themselves.

Reading the stories of these courageous men and women not only helps us discover the principles that we will use to guide our own lives but also teaches us about our black heritage and about America itself. It is crucial for us to know the heroes and heroines of our history and to realize that the price we paid in our struggle for equality in America was dear. But we must also understand that we have gotten as far as we have partly because America's democratic system and ideals made it possible.

We are still struggling with racism and prejudice. But the great men and women in this series are a tribute to the spirit of our democratic ideals and the system in which they have flourished. And that makes their stories special and worth knowing. ✦

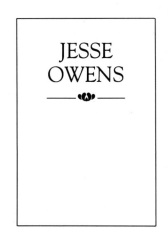

JESSE
OWENS

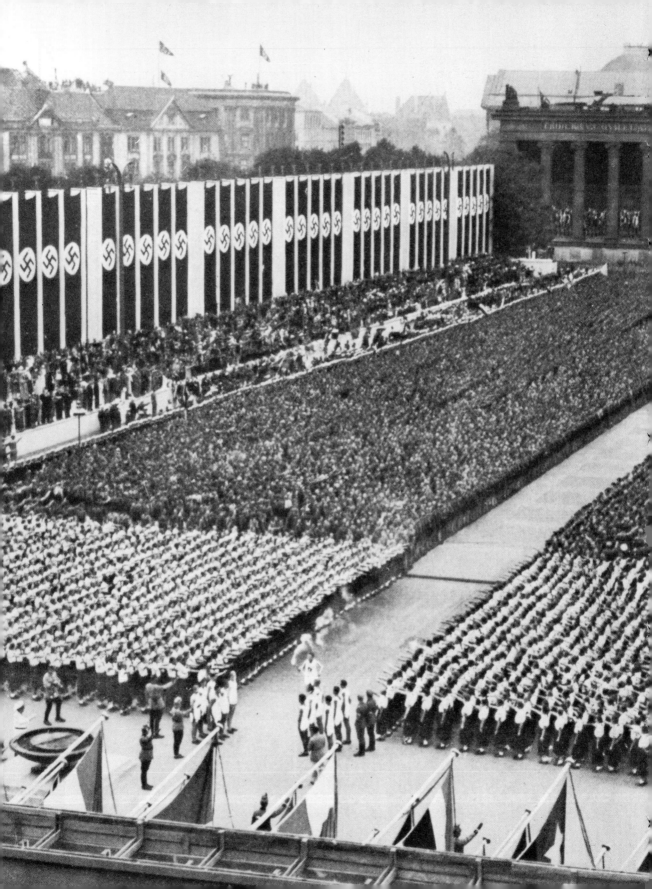

1

THE
NAZI
CHALLENGE

❦

ADOLF HITLER AWOKE on the rainy morning of August 1, 1936, looking forward to his grandest day yet as Germany's chancellor. He was to attend the opening ceremonies of the summer Olympics later that afternoon. The eleventh Games in modern history, the Olympic festival was slated to take place in his country's capital, Berlin, with 52 nations participating.

Three years earlier, shortly after he had come to power, Hitler said of the Games, "If Germany is to stand host to the entire world, her preparations must be complete and magnificent." To assure this, he had personally supervised a large part of the planning. With the help of 2,600 men, a stadium that could seat 100,000 spectators was erected out of stone on the western outskirts of the city. A swimming stadium, hockey arena, and dormitories for the athletes were also built. Century-old trees that bordered the city's avenues were dug up and moved to the athletic complex to make a park for the visitors.

A runner bearing the Olympic flame passes through the Lustgarten in Berlin, Germany, to mark the opening of the 1936 Summer Olympics. By staging the Games on a grander scale than the world had ever seen, German chancellor Adolf Hitler hoped to camouflage the evil intentions of his Third Reich from the festival's many visitors.

Adolf Hitler (standing in the car at left) leads a motorcade through the heart of Berlin on August 1, 1936, as he makes his way to the opening ceremonies of the Olympic Games. He expected his German athletes to dominate the action and was unfazed by the question repeatedly asked of him by the press: "Who have you got to beat Jesse Owens?"

Throughout the preparations, the Games were heavily promoted, often with colorful touches. The zeppelin *Hindenburg*, the world's largest airship, towed an Olympic flag across the Berlin sky. Thousands of people, from schoolchildren to soldiers, rehearsed for months, with marching bands and parading regiments slated to take part in the opening ceremonies. More than 3,000 runners were asked to carry the Olympic torch a kilometer each from Athens, Greece—the site of the first Olympic Games—to Berlin, so that the flame would arrive at the huge stadium just as the festivities were about to begin.

At precisely 3:00 P.M., a motorcade of sleek and powerful convertible limousines left Hitler's quarters, with the man dubbed the führer (German for the leader) in the head car. The procession traveled down streets lined with flags bearing the Nazi swastika emblem before turning onto the rain-slick boulevard leading to the Olympic stadium. A fanatical shout went up from the thousands of people lining the route.

Dressed in his military uniform, Hitler stood in the front seat, his eyes set straight ahead. "The Leader came by slowly in a shining car," wrote American novelist Thomas Wolfe, "a little dark man with a comic-opera moustache, erect and standing, moveless and unsmiling, with his hand upraised, palm outward, not in Nazi-wise salute, but straight up, in a gesture of blessing such as the Buddha or Messiahs use." Following the limousines and motorcycles came a runner carrying the Olympic torch on the last kilometer of its 10-day journey.

The ovation that greeted Hitler's arrival in the main stadium was nearly matched by the cheers for the approach of the Olympic torch. As soon as the runner lit the huge fire bowl in the stadium, the procession of the athletes began. Hitler and the 100,000 people surrounding him stood to salute the representatives of all the nations that had come

Twenty-eight thousand members of the Hitler Youth, Germany's national athletic organization for boys, and the Bund Deutscher Mädchen, a similar association for girls, take part in the opening ceremonies of the 1936 Games on May Field, outside the main Olympic stadium in Berlin. Regulated by the Nazi party, both organizations combined sports with politics.

to compete. With martial music blaring over loudspeakers, the athletes marched smartly around the track. Among them were blacks, Jews, Hispanics, Orientals, and Arabs, none of whom fit the Nazi model of a proper human being.

The German coaches had all but purged their Olympic team of any competitors who were not Aryan—native born, white, and non-Jewish. Hitler would have preferred that the other nations do the same. Yet if they saw fit to enter what he considered subhumans alongside his Aryan athletes, then his team would simply have to defeat them, proving to the world the strength of his nation of racially pure supermen.

Radio broadcasts and leaflets had blanketed Germany for months, promoting the brilliance of the nation's athletes, even as Jewish stars, born and raised in Germany, were hounded from the team. So the Games began, with Hitler's Aryans, cheered on by 100,000 spectators, facing off against everybody else. The cards, it seemed, were stacked. With the Germans on their home turf, the world was about to be taught a moral lesson.

Competition began the next day, on Sunday, August 2. The first event was the preliminary eliminations of the men's 100-meter dash, generally considered the most glamorous of the track-and-field events because the winner has the right to call himself "the world's fastest human." German fans held high hopes for their best runner, Erich Borchmeyer, who Americans thought looked more like a football player than a runner. But the Germans also had an eye out for the black American college student Jesse Owens, who held the world record in the 100-yard dash. As he stepped onto the rain-muddied track for his warm-ups, all eyes turned his way, wondering how the unassuming young man would do at this slightly longer distance.

Owens (far right) tries to keep warm on the first day of competition of the 1936 Olympics as he waits his turn in the 12th—and last—heat of the men's 100-meter run. Seated next to him are American sprinters Frank Wykoff (far left) and Ralph Metcalfe (second from right) and Swiss runner Paul Hánni.

Borchmeyer won his preliminary heat in a time of 10.7 seconds. An American sprinter, Frank Wykoff, bettered Borchmeyer's time by a hair in another heat.

Finally, just before noon, Owens got his chance. The hosts had furnished each sprinter with a silver hand shovel to help dig toe holes at the starting line (the aluminum-and-rubber starting blocks used by runners today were unheard-of then). Owens looked over the damp cinder track, which was already pocked and scarred by the feet of other runners, and got down on his knees to dig a foothold.

When the starter fired his gun, Owens shot off his mark, arms and legs pumping, even before the sound of the gun reached the upper seats of the stadium. In just a few steps he attained full speed. He ran with a fluid, easy stride; his eyes looked straight ahead, as if his only opponent were the tape stretched across the track fewer than 100 meters away. His feet hardly seemed to touch the ground.

Owens finished yards ahead of his closest competitor, coasting effortlessly across the finish line in a time that equaled the world record of 10.3 seconds. The crowd went wild. Even fervent Nazis could not ignore the speed of this young man.

Owens in a second-round heat of the men's 100-meter run, crossing the finish line for an unofficial world record of 10.2 seconds. His outstanding performance in the event marked the start of his dominance in the 1936 Olympic Games.

That afternoon, Owens ran in the second round of heats. Again, he made it look easy. No other runner even came close during the race. And this time Owens shaved a tenth of a second off his earlier standard, breaking the world mark. The judges decided that his time had been aided by the wind, however, so they could not award him the record.

That did not matter to Owens or to the crowd. He would run again the next day, and the next. Who could say how fast he might run in the 100-meter semifinals and finals? It was even possible that the 100-meter dash was not his best event. Didn't he also hold world records in the 220-yard dash and the long jump? Moreover, he was clearly at the top of his form, prepared to trounce all comers beneath the gray skies of Berlin.

German youngsters seeking autographs eagerly surrounded Owens on the way back to his room. On the very first day of the Olympic Games, he had proved a sensation. This must have come as a rude surprise to Hitler. These Games were to have been the führer's showpiece. Blond, blue-eyed white men and women from Germany were supposed to capture the spotlight.

But one man changed all that. One American upstaged Adolf Hitler at what was meant to be his greatest glory. One American athlete performed as no one has since, captivating a worldwide audience. One black American athlete made a laughingstock of the Nazis' racist notions, throwing Hitler's challenge right back into his mustachioed face. That man was Jesse Owens.

Within the span of a week, Owens would become an international hero, prompting people everywhere to ask the questions that must have been on the führer's lips as he sat in his special box and watched the races being run: Who is this incredible athlete? Where did he come from? What is he like? How can anyone be so good?

2

"FIGHTING
THE
WIND"

❦

JAMES CLEVELAND OWENS was born on September 12, 1913, in Oakville, Alabama—unimaginably far from the lights and fanfare of Berlin. Nicknamed J. C., he was the tenth (and last) child of Henry and Mary Emma Owens. He had six brothers—Prentice, Johnson, Henry, Ernest, Quincy, and Sylvester—and three sisters, Ida, Josephine, and Lillie.

Like thousands of families, black and white, throughout the South, the Owenses were sharecroppers. This meant that a local landowner, Albert Owens, allowed them to live in a beat-up house on his property and use his farm equipment in exchange for their hard work and half the season's crop from the land they farmed. The Owenses sold the other half of the crop, and with the little bit of money they earned they bought clothing and a few basic supplies.

A predominantly white community of 1,000 residents, Oakville was situated along a red dirt road amid the rolling hills and tall pines of northern Alabama. Most of the Owenses' neighbors were sharecroppers, too. They plowed, behind a mule, the fields

---

Owens spent his early years in north-central Alabama, on a sharecropper's plantation much like the one shown here. "It was more dozens and dozens of farms," he later said of Oakville, the community in which he was raised, "than a real town."

The son of former slaves, Owens's father, Henry, barely managed to scratch out a living in Oakville as a sharecropper. According to Jesse, the senior Owens "had no more earthly possessions than [a] mule and the shredded clothes he wore to shield him from the sun."

in the spring, hoed the long rows of corn and cotton throughout the scorching summer, then picked cotton from sunup to sundown during the backbreaking two-week-long harvest in the fall. Struggling to make their harvest money stretch through the winter, they fretted and prayed.

With so much work to be done, all the Owens children were expected to pitch in. But the youngest son, J. C., gave his parents fits. He was small and sickly, and it was a trial to nurse him through one cold winter after another, especially because his father could not afford to buy any medicine or pay for a doctor. As the drafty old house rattled with every icy blast, little J. C., wrapped in soft cotton feed sacks in front of the stove, coughed and sweated and cried with pneumonia for weeks at a time.

As if that were not enough, terrifying boils appeared on J. C.'s chest and legs. His father had to hold the crying child while his mother practiced surgery in her own home, carving the boils out of his flesh with a red-hot kitchen knife. Years later, in his autobiography, *Jesse*, Owens recounted one of those doctoring sessions in all its harrowing detail: "Real pain is when you don't have any choice any more whether to cry or not, and then maybe you don't even cry because it wouldn't help. I always hated to go to sleep at night, but now for the first time in my life I wanted to pass out. Something inside wouldn't let me. All I felt was the knife going deeper, around and around, trying to cut that thing loose, all I saw were the tears running down my father's face, all I heard was my own voice—but like it was somebody else's from far-off—moaning, 'Aww, Momma, no . . .' "

Through sheer will and the determination of his long-suffering parents, little J. C. somehow survived these brushes with death. And by the age of six, he was well enough to walk the nine miles to school with his brothers and sisters.

School amounted to a one-room shack that doubled on Sunday as the Baptist church for the blacks of the area. The teacher was anybody who had the time and the inclination. During spring planting and at harvesttime, students worked the fields instead of arithmetic problems. In spite of all the drawbacks and interruptions, J. C. learned to read and write.

Meanwhile, his parents struggled to make a better life. First, they moved their family to a larger farm in Oakville, where they worked 50 acres of land. Nevertheless, sharecroppers rarely expected to earn much money, and the Owenses were no exception. The children endured the hard times by concentrating on happier moments: fishing, raccoon hunts, swimming, berry picking, games of hide-and-seek, and schoolboy pranks. "We used to have a lot of fun," Owens recalled. "We never had any problems. We always ate. The fact that we didn't have steak? Who had steak?" His family, like most sharecroppers, did not think of themselves as poor because all their neighbors were poor, too.

With hard work and good weather, a family could pick enough berries for jams and collect enough windfallen apples, pears, and peaches to last through the winter. They canned tomatoes and beans from their garden and slaughtered a hog after harvesttime. So even though the Owenses did not have much money, there was usually enough to eat.

And with all that, there was time for play. It was in the low hills of Alabama that J. C. first began to run. He recalled in his autobiography that even as thin and sickly as he was, "I always loved running. I wasn't very good at it, but I loved it because it was something you could do all by yourself, and under your own power. You could go in any direction, fast

Mary Emma Owens proved to be the chief source of inspiration in Jesse's life. Unlike her husband, who had become resigned to a life of poverty, she urged her children to dream of greater things and to work hard to attain them.

Around 1920, the Owenses, like many other southern blacks searching for a better way of life, gave up sharecropping and moved to the industrial North. They settled in Cleveland's East Side ghetto (below), which Owens said was "a better world . . . most always" than the one his family had known in Alabama.

or slow as you wanted, fighting the wind if you felt like it, seeking out new sights just on the strength of your feet and the courage of your lungs."

As the Owens family continued to eke out an existence from the red dirt of Oakville, prospects of better opportunities beckoned at last. One of J. C.'s sisters, Lillie, had moved to Cleveland, Ohio, and she soon wrote home that she had found work there earning more money than she had ever seen before. She begged her parents to pull up roots and join her in this worker's paradise.

Henry and Mary Emma Owens, however, did not jump at the chance to leave their tattered farmhouse amid the cotton fields. The Owens family had roots in northern Alabama that ran back for a century, into slavery days. They had never known anything but farm life. As fellow members of the Baptist church, their friends and family spread for miles around in the northern Alabama hills.

J. C.'s father understood particularly well how ill equipped he was to face urban life. He had never learned to read or write or even to calculate the value of the cotton he harvested. He was a good farmer and a well-respected deacon of the church, but none of that would matter in the big city.

Even so, his wife approached him with their daughter's letter in her hand and a determined sparkle in her eye. She pointed out that the family was not faring too well in the rural South. A move to Cleveland was not such a gamble.

J. C.'s father never stood a chance against his wife's arguments. When he reminded her how unschooled he was, she asked him if he wanted his 10 children to grow up just as ignorant. When he told her how he would miss the farm life, she waved her hand through their dark, unpainted rooms, showed him the all-but-empty kitchen shelves, ran a finger through the holes in her apron, and laughed.

For Mary Emma Owens, the family had nothing to lose and everything to gain from catching the first train north. And when J. C. turned nine years old, they sent him down the road to sell their mule to a neighbor. With that money, they all bought train tickets, and as their youngest child later recalled, he stood with his folks on the platform at the Oakville station and asked, "Where's the train gonna take us, Momma?" She answered only, "It's gonna take us to a better life."

That better life, however, lay a little more than a train ride away. The Owens family moved into the only apartment they could afford, in a ghetto neighborhood on Cleveland's East Side. Back in the country, the view beyond the windows of their house had expanded for miles across open fields beneath the limitless blue sky of Alabama. In the city, their windows opened onto bedraggled alleys and the walls of the building next door. Emma Owens more often than not kept her curtains closed.

But now that she had convinced the family to move north, J. C.'s mother was not about to forget her dream. She took jobs all over town, cleaning houses and washing laundry, and put her daughters to work doing the same. The older sons took jobs in a steel mill, where the foremen appreciated the strength and endurance the Owens boys had developed in the fields. J. C., too young for such grueling labor, found a part-time job polishing shoes and sweeping up in a cobbler's shop.

But for Henry Owens, who was in his forties, the move north had perhaps come too late. Worn down by a lifetime on the farm, he could not keep up with his sons in the mill and had to settle for whatever part-time work he could find. Still, for the first time in his life, his labor earned him a paycheck. At the end of the week, the family pooled its money to buy luxuries they had only imagined in the South: new shoes, new clothes, and good, sturdy furniture.

The bustling city swirled about them. Mill work proved exhausting, closed in, run by time clocks and strict supervisors. Shysters waited on every corner to cheat a man out of his wages. Around the dinner table in their ghetto home, the Owens family acted out a story repeated in millions of urban households all over the country during the first half of the 20th century—that of rural people in crowded apartments, bewildered and harried by their new environment, weighing in their minds the advantages and disadvantages of the move they had made to the city.

And if the working life seemed worlds apart from the farm, 10-year-old J. C. discovered that Bolton Elementary School was just as far from the one-room schoolhouse back home in Oakville. Everything at Bolton ran in a businesslike fashion. For example, when the busy teacher asked for J. C.'s name, she misunderstood his slow southern drawl and wrote it down as "Jesse." Afraid to interrupt her on his first day of school, the youngster took his seat without comment, and for the rest of his life he was called Jesse instead of J. C.

Unsure of how much schooling her new student had previously received, the teacher assigned Jesse to

While a student at Fairmount Junior High School in Cleveland, Owens formally began his career as a track athlete. He encountered little success in school meets, however, because he had not yet overcome, as he later put it, "the instinct to slack off, give in to the pain and give less than your best, and wish to win through things falling right, or your opponents not doing their best, instead of going to the limit, past your limit, where victory is always found. Because it's victory over yourself."

first grade, where he towered over his younger class-mates. But the little school in Oakville had taught him enough, so he quickly moved up to another class. Even so, he was a couple of years older and a few inches taller than the other children in his classroom.

Bolton, like the community it served, was a racially mixed school. Jesse soon made friends with children from all over the world—Poles, Hungarians, Greeks, Italians, and Chinese. He ran himself ragged exploring his new neighborhood, which seemed so much larger, more exciting, and more dangerous than

At the age of 15, Owens began dating Minnie Ruth Solomon, who later became his wife. "I fell in love with her some the first time we ever talked," he said, "and a little bit more every time after that."

the fields of Alabama. His imagination ran wild. In Cleveland, it seemed, all that limited anyone was how well their legs could keep up with their dreams. For children like Jesse—more energetic, more inquisitive, less set in their ways than their parents were—even a large city's ghetto could seem like a wonderland.

Jesse Owens spent the next three years of his life that way. In addition to working at the cobbler's shop, he held jobs in a greenhouse watering plants and as a grocery store delivery boy. The northern winters, however, kept him in bed fighting it out with pneumonia for weeks. When the time came for him to enter junior high school, Owens probably felt that he knew all about city life. No longer the awkward southern hick, he stayed out of trouble, went to church on Sunday with his parents, and played a mean game of stickball.

Then, at Fairmount Junior High School, Owens's life gradually began to diverge from that of his playground friends. All in one week he met the two people who would change his life. Each in his or her own way would show him a glimpse of a larger world than the one he knew on Cleveland's windy streets and then dare him to chase it.

The first person was a pretty young girl named Minnie Ruth Solomon. Owens must have grinned when she told him her parents had been sharecroppers in Georgia and had just recently moved north to try their hand in the city. It is easy to imagine 14-year-old Jesse, a playful glint in his eye, offering to show her the town.

As Owens recalled in adulthood, for him it was love at first sight: "She was unusual because even though I knew her family was as poor as ours, nothing she said or did seemed touched by that. Or by prejudice. Or by anything the world said or did. It was as if she had something inside her that somehow made

Owens with his first and foremost track coach, Charles Riley. "I'd noticed him watching me for a year or so," Owens said of his junior high school physical education teacher, "especially when we'd play games where there was running or jumping."

all that not count. I fell in love with her some the first time we ever talked, and a little bit more every time after that until I thought I couldn't love her more than I did. And when I felt that way, I asked her to marry me . . . and she said she would." Jesse and Ruth were still too young for marriage, but their puppy love would grow.

The second important person Owens met at junior high was a short, skinny man with a whistle around his neck: Charles Riley, who coached the school's track team. Who knows what the wiry Irishman saw in the happy-go-lucky kid from Alabama? He certainly was not the strongest, the fastest, or even the healthiest student in school. But Riley may have guessed at his potential, or maybe he just wanted to help Owens build up his lungs to fend off his frequent attacks of pneumonia. Whatever the reason, Riley called Owens into his office one day and asked if he would be interested in running a little after school.

Thus began a career that would rewrite the records of track and field, shake up a dictator, and make the name *Jesse Owens* a household word worldwide.

3

"FOUR YEARS FROM NEXT FRIDAY"

❧

THE TEACHERS AT Fairmount Junior High School knew that most of their students would never go on to high school. In the East Cleveland ghetto, bright youngsters had to grow up fast, helping their families earn a living any way they could. So classes skimmed over English, history, and mathematics, concentrating instead on the kinds of lessons that might help students find and hold jobs as laborers. Boys learned to use tools; girls were taught how to type and cook. Arriving on time, dressing cleanly, and following instructions meant more than test scores did.

Jesse Owens thrived under these conditions. Friendly, compliant, a fastidious dresser, he had never been a whiz at textbooks. Fairmount rewarded his strengths and did not hammer too hard at his weaknesses.

Meanwhile, a passion began to occupy Owens's imagination "so completely," he said, "that whole days would pass when I didn't think of anything else." He began to think of himself as a runner. Coach Charles Riley set up a training schedule for Owens, even though he was too young to compete on the school's track team. Because the youngster held part-time jobs after school, he asked the coach if it would be all right to train in the morning. Riley must have reasoned that if this skinny but eager student was willing to push himself so hard, then he could not

A teenage Owens during his days at East Technical High School in Cleveland. He enrolled at the school in 1930 and quickly became one of its most popular students.

say no. So, most days at dawn the two met, one sipping coffee and watching while the other stretched and jumped and ran.

It was not long before Owens began to look up to Riley almost as a second father. He even called the Irishman "Pop." The coach made sure Owens ate well, bringing him breakfast from his own table or inviting him to dinner with his family. He used their training sessions not only to build up the runner's legs and lungs but to build character as well. Riley told all of his teenage charges not to expect immediate results but always to train for "four years from next Friday." Steady, gradual improvement was the goal.

Riley may have been the first man Owens had ever met who challenged him to test his limitations. Having inherited from his mother the drive to achieve, Owens found in Riley a teacher who woke up early every day to hammer the point home that the biggest obstacle anyone has to overcome is within one's own head. Riley said that a man has to push himself every day, winning out over the tricks his mind plays on itself, in order to reach his potential. Yet he was not one to preach. He taught by quiet example and encouragement.

In the 1920s, most world-class sprinters tried to power down the track, furiously pumping their arms and legs. Riley thought this was unnatural. One day he took Owens to a racetrack to see the relaxed grace of the thoroughbreds as they ran, their hooves seeming to barely touch the turf, their eyes always looking forward, a study in speed. He told Owens and his other students to mimic the horses, to run as if the track were on fire, keeping each foot on the ground for as little time as possible. These characteristics became the hallmark of Owens's running style throughout his career and, through his example, revolutionized the way sprinters everywhere learned to run.

For a year, Coach Riley put Owens through his paces. Then one day he decided to time Owens at the distance of 100 yards. When Owens flew past the coach 11 seconds later, all Riley could do was stand there in openmouthed astonishment. He asked Owens to run the distance again, and again the runner clocked in at 11 seconds—unbelievably fast for a 15 year old. It was time to suit this youngster up for the team.

Riley knew that with such speed Owens would make a good jumper. He signed Owens up to compete not only in the 100-yard and 220-yard dashes but also

"Every morning, just like in Alabama," Owens said of his high school days, "I got up with the sun, ate my breakfast even before my mother and sisters and brothers, and went to school, winter, spring, and fall alike to run and jump and bend my body this way and that for Mr. Charles Riley."

Owens (second from left) in the spring of 1932, when he was coming into his own as a runner. By winning this 100-meter race at the Northern Ohio Amateur Athletic Union Track-and-Field Championships, he automatically qualified for the quarterfinals of that year's Olympic Trials.

in the long jump and high jump. Sometimes, Riley entered him in the hurdles or the 440-yard run, guessing that these races would make the sprints seem easier. Owens quickly repaid his coach's confidence. In his first year on the track team, he broke the world record for junior high school students in the high jump and long jump. When Charlie Paddock, an Olympic gold medalist in the 100-meter dash, came to the school to deliver a speech, Riley introduced him to Owens. From the moment the two shook hands, Owens's only dream was to reach the Olympics.

But as Owens trained ever harder, life at home threatened to dash his dream. His father broke a leg when he was hit by a taxicab, and because of the injury he lost his job. Jesse's brothers, one after the other, were laid off from the steel mill, and when they could not pay their rent they moved their wives and children into their parents' already crowded house. These were the years of the Great Depression, when the nation's economy all but collapsed. Poor people, holding down the most tenuous of jobs, took the brunt of the hard times. Millions of workers all over the United States found themselves penniless and hungry, standing on food lines.

The pressure must have been great for 17-year-old Jesse to drop out of school and do what he could to help the family make ends meet. Credit must go to his mother, who, despite her tough days washing laundry for pennies, convinced her son to continue his education. In 1930, Owens enrolled at East Technical High School, a few blocks from his house. He tried out for the football and basketball teams but soon gave them up when they cut into his running time.

The track coach at East Tech, Edgar Weil, was not the inspiring innovator that Coach Riley had been. But, luckily for Owens, Weil soon asked Riley to be his assistant, and under Riley's continued tutelage Owens came into his own. In the spring of 1932, during his junior year, he proved so dominant a competitor that one newspaper called him a "one-man team." That estimation was not far off the mark. Owens often scored more than half the points for his whole team at track meets.

But again private life intruded on Owens's ambitions. His girlfriend, Ruth, reported one day that she had become pregnant. The two hastily eloped to Pennsylvania in a car driven by a friend, David Albritten. The young couple claimed that they were married in Erie by a justice of the peace. It is more likely, however, that Owens and Solomon did not go through with the wedding, for no marriage license exists from that time. In any event, when the two lovers returned to Cleveland, they faced the wrath of their parents. Ruth's father swore never to let Owens see his daughter again.

Owens could do nothing but concentrate on his running. That summer, he took a big step toward realizing his dream, traveling to Northwestern University to try out for the U.S. Olympic team. But 1932 was not to be the year of Jesse Owens; he did not make the team. In both the 100-yard and 220-yard dashes, he lost to Marquette University sprinter Ralph Metcalfe, who went on to win silver and bronze medals at the 1932 Olympic Games in Los Angeles. Metcalfe was a powerhouse runner of the old school. He and Owens would become firm friends—and arch-rivals—in the years ahead.

In the trials for the 1932 U.S. Olympic team, Owens got as far as the midwestern preliminaries, where he lost in the 100- and 200-meter races to Ralph Metcalfe (left), then the top American sprinter. Metcalfe later won a bronze medal in the 200 meters and a silver medal in the 100 meters at the 1932 Games in Los Angeles, finishing second in the shorter race to teammate Eddie Tolan (second from left).

When the Olympics were over, some of the run-ners toured the United States, holding demonstration track meets. It must have come as some consolation to Owens that he won the 100-yard and 220-yard dashes and even finished second behind the 1932 Olympic gold medalist in the long jump, Edward Gor-don, when the squad came through Cleveland. But no matter how Owens felt about his performances, he gained valuable experience in competing on an international level.

Owens could not keep his mind entirely on his running, however. On August 8, 16-year-old Ruth gave birth to their baby. A healthy little girl, she was given the name Gloria Shirley. With this, Ruth's high school days were over. She dropped out of school and took a job in a beauty parlor. But she continued to live with her parents, who still would not let Jesse in the house.

By refusing him the responsibilities of fatherhood, the Solomons, perhaps unwittingly, did Owens a

One of the few flaws in Owens's running technique during the early portion of his track career was his start, which was not as explosive as he would have liked. He reme-died the problem by making a few adjustments in his takeoff stance and improving his concentration as the starter was about to fire the gun.

favor. Now he could enter his senior year of high school and continue his track-and-field career. As a testament to his popularity, his East Tech classmates (95 percent of whom were white) voted him student body president. As the high scorer and natural leader of the track team, he became squad captain as well.

Owens repaid his admirers with electrifying performances, not losing a race all year. Though he never deliberately drew attention to himself, he was so clearly head and shoulders above the other competitors that all eyes stayed on him, whether he was running a race or landing in the long-jump pit. On May 20, 1933, he concluded his high school career in typically splendid fashion. At the state interscholastic finals that day, he broke the world record for high school students in the long jump, sailing 24 feet, 3⅙ inches.

Then, in June, at the National Interscholastic Meet in Chicago, Owens eclipsed even his own standards. In the 100-yard dash, he tied the world record of 9.4 seconds. In the long jump, he improved his best leap by a remarkable six inches. And then, in the 220-yard dash, he ran a blazing 20.7 seconds, breaking the world record.

The town fathers back home in Cleveland were quick to honor the city's new favorite son. They organized a victory parade as soon as Owens got home. One can only imagine the pride of Henry and Mary Emma Owens as they were helped into the backseat of a convertible, flanking their son, for the slow-moving procession along the broad streets downtown. In the car directly behind theirs rode Charles Riley. Perhaps he guessed that this would be only the first of many victory parades for his favorite student. And somewhere in the crowd one can picture Ruth, holding a daughter who was not quite one year old, helping the baby wave at her father's car going by.

Owens at the age of 19, showing his mother the four medals he won at his final high school meet, the National Interscholastic Championship in Chicago. Among his achievements at this June 1933 tournament were setting a new world record in the 220-yard dash and equaling the world mark in the 100-yard dash.

When the procession stopped at City Hall, the mayor of Cleveland joined several council members in praising the young athlete, happy to discover a hero during such difficult times. They predicted a grand future at whatever college he chose to attend.

Owens let none of the fanfare go to his head. He drove a hard bargain in negotiating with the big midwestern schools that were clamoring for his talents. During the summer, Coach Riley drove Owens all

Cleveland mayor Ray Miller congratulates Owens in June 1933 on his accomplishments at the National Interscholastic Championship. Owens's father (third from left) and mother (far right) were on hand at City Hall for the festivities.

the way to the University of Michigan to tour the campus. But in the end, Owens elected to stay close to home. Ohio State University, in the state capital of Columbus, won the budding star.

In those days, colleges did not give athletic scholarships. Instead, they offered easy jobs at good wages to help students pay their way. After school each day, Owens would have to run a freight elevator at the State House. Having held much more strenuous jobs most of his life, he quickly agreed. Owens even secured a custodial job on campus for his father, but Henry Owens did not have it in him to pull up roots again. He chose to stay home in Cleveland and appreciate his son's exploits long distance.

There was one major hitch in all these arrangements. Owens had just slipped by with a D average in high school, and his report card failed to impress the administrators at Ohio State. The coaches got around this difficulty by having Owens take special tests over the summer. When he passed these, the last door opened.

With the next few years decided upon, Owens could tie up loose ends at home. For spending money, he pumped gas at a filling station. At long last, the Solomons gave in to their daughter's pleas and allowed Owens to visit after work each day. And on weekends, Riley drove him in his Model T to track meets. Once, they even drove as far as Toronto, Canada, for an international competition.

With autumn approaching, the old coach prepared to say farewell to his surrogate son. Pop Riley had started Owens out on the road to glory, instilling in him a will to win and a humility toward the tasks that would face him in the years ahead. Owens was 19 years old, already arguably the world's fastest human. The rest would be up to him. ✺

4

COUNTDOWN
TO THE
OLYMPICS

Owens at a training session with his track coach at Ohio State University, Larry Snyder. "He was constantly on me," Owens said, "about the job that I was to do and the responsibility that I had upon the campus. And how I must be able to carry myself because people were looking."

JESSE OWENS WAS among the handful of blacks that enrolled in an American university in 1933, when the Great Depression caused an unusually low percentage of high school graduates to enter college. Nevertheless, at Ohio State, a school where athletes—particularly football players—are treated like conquering heroes, he fit right in. The coaches made sure he signed up for easy courses, knowing that his secondary schooling had not been the best. And the job running a freight elevator was even easier. Because freight was rarely delivered during his shift at night, he had hours of free time to study on the job. Finally, Owens learned that he could make extra cash traveling about the state on weekends, giving speeches to help promote the school. At that rate, he later recalled, he not only paid for his education but saved enough to send regular checks home to his mother and to help Ruth raise their baby.

Meanwhile, every day, Owens trained for the track season. In January 1934, without ever having run a race in college, he was named to the Amateur Athletic Union (AAU) All-American Track Team. Everything seemed to go well during the first semester but his grades. East Technical High School in Cleveland had done little to prepare Owens for a college curriculum, and having never learned how to study, he quickly fell behind his classmates. At the begin-

Not permitted to join Ohio State's varsity squad in 1933–34 because he was still a freshman, Owens (far right) participated instead in freshman meets and regional tournaments, including this February 1934 contest in New York City that was won by Ralph Metcalfe (second from right).

ning of the spring semester, he was put on academic probation and ordered to bring up his grades.

Ohio State's track coach was a young man named Larry Snyder. A character builder as well as a coach, he must have seemed to Owens like a younger, peppier, more ambitious version of Pop Riley. Snyder liked the natural running style Owens had developed in high school, but he believed there was still room for improvement. In the sprints, he concentrated on getting Owens to relax even more—he tended to tense his upper body and arms—and he taught the freshman a more compact crouch at the starting line, which would help him uncoil quickly into a full-speed run. In the long jump, Snyder showed the freshman how to "run through" the air, pumping his arms and legs for more distance as he flew. A dedicated student when it came to track and field, Owens practiced these new techniques with a diligence he rarely applied to his schoolbooks. (Such an attitude toward his classwork would ultimately hurt him in later years.)

According to collegiate rules, Owens, like all incoming students, was not eligible to compete on a varsity team until his sophomore year. After another summer spent pumping gas back home in Cleveland, he traded in his job running the elevator for a more prestigious position as a page for state legislators in the capitol. When he joined the varsity track squad later in the year, the refinements Coach Snyder had taught him began immediately to pay dividends. On February 9, 1935, in his first Big Ten Conference meet, Owens won 3 out of 4 events, placing second in the 70-yard low hurdles. It was plain to all concerned that he would be able to compete successfully on the college level.

Owens must have guessed that he was reaching the top of his form. For seven intense years, he had trained to run and jump with the best. But at the

Big Ten Championships in Ann Arbor, Michigan, on May 25, 1935, he shocked even himself. In the space of 45 minutes, Jesse Owens broke 5 world records and tied another. This feat has never been equaled; it is still considered the greatest single performance in the history of track and field.

Owens's teammates could not believe their eyes. They had seen him wearing hot packs on his back all week after falling down a flight of steps at school. When Coach Snyder, wary of aggravating the injury, wanted to bench him for the meet, they had overheard Owens pleading for the chance to run. Owens later said that he knew he would be all right when he first crouched down for the 100-yard dash. Miraculously, the pain seemed to disappear. And after the starter's pistol sounded, Owens did the same, blazing effortlessly into the lead and tying the world record of 9.4 seconds.

In the 220-yard dash, Owens shaved four-tenths of a second off his previous best time, reclaiming the

By his sophomore year, Owens (far left) had become one of the best-known sprinters in the nation. He is shown here in February 1935, winning the 60-yard dash at the Millrose Games in New York City's Madison Square Garden.

world record. He was also awarded the international record for the slightly shorter distance of 200 meters without having to run that race. Then, in his worst event, the 220-yard low hurdles, he breezed to a new standard of 22.6 seconds. In this race, he finished 10 yards ahead of his nearest competitor. Again, he was allowed the low-hurdles record for the shorter international distance of 200 meters.

It took just one leap for Owens to break the world record in the long jump. At his request, a friend placed a handkerchief beside the pit at the 26-foot mark. Owens soared past the handkerchief, landing 8¼ inches beyond it. This astounding leap was not equaled for 25 years. After such a performance, Owens then took his coach's advice and chose not to try for a longer distance.

Owens at work in 1935: pumping gas at a service station in Cleveland (right) and as a page in Ohio's State House (opposite).

Immediately, autograph seekers and reporters mobbed the new champion. Owens posed for photographers, shook hands, and signed his name all the way back to the dressing room. So many well-wishers crowded the door there that he had to escape through a back window. In the parking lot, patiently waiting in that old Model T, sat Coach Charles Riley, who had cheered with everyone else as Owens rewrote the record books.

As they took the long drive back to Riley's house for a celebratory dinner, the old coach quietly prepared his protégé for the fame that was to come. He

In addition to the sprints, Owens frequently competed in the long jump (right) and the 220-yard low hurdles (opposite). He considered the hurdles to be his weakest event.

explained that life would be different from now on. Owens had been a contender; but in one day he had become a star. Now the top runners in the world would be gunning for him. Fans would surround him. Every move he made would be scrutinized by the press.

No doubt the young runner listened respectfully to Riley's thoughtful advice. But neither man could have guessed that the success they had cultivated for so long would soon be challenged from four different directions. Although none of these challenges came on the track, any one of them might have ended Owens's drive toward the Olympics.

The first challenge arrived in the beautiful person of Quincella Nickerson, a wealthy socialite who took the runner's arm one night in June 1935 after a meet in Los Angeles. Imagine the response back in Cleveland, Ohio, at the Solomon household when the grinning faces of this glamorous couple appeared in the local papers, captioned with hints of a wedding engagement.

Ruth Solomon caught up with Owens by telephone when the track team reached Lincoln, Ne-

Owens (left) at the Big Ten Championships in May 1935, setting a new world record in the 220-yard low hurdles. He usually compensated for his less-than-perfect hurdling technique by soaring rather than skimming over the barriers.

braska. Whatever she told him, he promptly went out and lost all his races at the AAU Championships the next day, July 4. Then he caught the first train back to Cleveland. In the Solomons' living room, which had been off limits to him for so long, he and Ruth were married that afternoon. The event was covered in newspapers nationwide. And the next morning, a chastened young husband, still burning from his first brush with celebrity, left for the East Coast and the relative peace and quiet of track meets there.

Shaken by it all, Owens lost his races to a fine runner named Eulace Peacock. Then he returned home to his new family and his summer job at the filling station, reading in the papers that Peacock now seemed to be the front-runner in the race for the Olympics.

There was no rest for the weary. AAU officials called Owens back to Columbus in August, threatening to bar him from competition. He had received checks totaling $159 during the summer from his page's job at the State House. Part of the sum was for travel expenses, and Owens had used the money to pay for his trip to California. To the AAU, the job seemed suspiciously like a cover-up for an outright athletic scholarship. Owens gave back the money, but it took all the persuasiveness of Ohio State University administrators and Ohio lawmakers to convince the AAU to drop its charges.

When his junior year got underway, Owens received yet another slap in the face. Those same university officials who had argued his case so convincingly just weeks before now suspended him from the track team for the winter season. The reason? Poor grades. They threatened to cut the world-record holder in six events from the team unless he hit the books hard.

If that was not enough, world politics impinged on the young runner, too. The Olympic Games were scheduled to begin in less than a year, in Berlin, Germany. But stories had begun to circulate about German mistreatment of Jews, blacks, Catholics, and political dissidents. Many of the nation's leading newspapers were calling for an American boycott of the Olympics in protest of Adolf Hitler's discriminatory policies, and the AAU made a tentative decision to keep American athletes out of the games.

All that winter, as Owens, unable to compete with his teammates, trained on his own, he could not be sure if he would be granted the opportunity to achieve his grand dream of reaching the Olympics. And worst of all, there was nothing he could do about it. The decision would be made by men in business suits, far from the playing fields.

It must have been a terrible time for the 20-year-old Owens, who faced pressure from all sides. But he remembered the teachings of Coach Riley—to challenge himself, to do his best—and he concentrated on those tasks that were within his control. Gradually, his grades came up, and by the time Owens rejoined the track team for the spring season he had run himself into the best shape of his life.

Against the University of Wisconsin on May 16, just 10 weeks prior to the Olympic Games, Owens ran the 100-yard dash in 9.3 seconds, breaking the world record. While his archrival Eulace Peacock struggled with a hamstring injury, Owens piled up victory after victory, all leading to the Olympic Trials in New York City on June 11 and 12. After an agreeable visit with German chancellor Adolf Hitler, AAU officials had decided that it would be all right for American athletes to compete in Berlin after all. The last barrier to Owens's dream had fallen. Now, after what must have seemed the darkest time since

Owens in July 1935 with his friend Eulace Peacock, who went on to defeat Owens five times in the next nine months. A hamstring injury prevented Peacock from making the 1936 U.S. Olympic team.

Owens performing at the Midwest regional tryouts for the 1936 U.S. Olympic team in the 100-meter run (above, far left) and the long jump (opposite). He wound up qualifying for the squad in those two events as well as in the 200-meter sprint.

his boyhood illnesses in Alabama, the door stood open for him.

At the Olympic Trials, Owens breezed to victory in the 100-meter and 200-meter dashes and in the long jump. His schoolboy pal David Albritten, also a teammate at Ohio State, made the team as a high jumper. Ralph Metcalfe, the 1932 medalist who had

beaten Owens in the trials that same year, also gained
a berth. These were 3 of the 19 black athletes who
would compete for the United States in the 1936
Olympics, 4 times the number who had made the
team 4 years earlier. The big disappointment: Eulace
Peacock. Hampered by his hamstring injury, he finished out of the running at the trials.

Owens married his childhood sweetheart, Minnie Ruth Solomon, on July 5, 1935, in her parents' home.

The night following the trials, Owens joined the other Olympians at a celebratory feast in Manhattan. There he was surprised and honored to find himself seated beside the legendary baseball slugger Babe Ruth. As Owens later recalled, Ruth wasted no time in asking, "You gonna win at the Olympics, Jesse?"

Owens replied, "Gonna try."

"Everybody tries," Ruth said. "I succeed. Wanna know why?"

Owens nodded.

"Because I know I'm going to hit a home run just about every time I swing that friggin' bat. I'm surprised when I *don't!* And that isn't all there is to it. Because I know it, the pitchers, *they* know it too."

Owens grinned at the supreme confidence of the baseball hero. And he did not fail to recognize the good advice hidden in the blustering anecdote. Sometimes, it is not enough to *want* to win. Sometimes, you have to *know* that you will. Owens took the Babe's advice with him on board the S.S. *Manhattan* when it departed for Berlin three days later.

Every kind of distraction awaited Owens during the week-long voyage, from heavy gourmet meals to Hollywood starlets who vied for his arm on the dance floor. To at least one of the Olympians, the distractions proved too much. The beautiful backstroke champion Eleanor Holm Jarrett partied her way to Berlin—and lost her chance to compete when a chaperon discovered her drunk on champagne one morning. Owens was careful to avoid all the premature celebrating. He kept his mind on his destination, performing calisthenics and watching what he ate, while getting to know his fellow Olympians.

There was a lot of time, too, for thinking over all he had been through, for thrilling to the fact that his wildest dream was about to come true. As Pop Riley had said, "Run to beat yourself." As Babe Ruth had suggested, "Know you will win." He would test both of these axioms, to their limit, in the Olympic Games. 🐾

All set to make a big noise: Owens in his New York hotel room in mid-July 1936, just before sailing with the U.S. Olympic team to Europe for the start of the Games.

5

THE DREAM
COME TRUE

❦

WHEN THE OLYMPIC Games began on August 1, 1936, German chancellor Adolf Hitler had been running his nation for a little more than three years. In that brief amount of time, he had raised the nation from a poor and broken-spirited country, beaten and divided by the Great War of 1914–18 (what is now called World War I), to a position of power in the world. He had put his unemployed countrymen to work building the first superhighways anyone had ever seen. These were broad and straight concrete roads he called autobahns, on which the powerful cars of the 1930s could run flat out, with no speed limit at all.

The skies of Nazi Germany were ruled by enormous hydrogen-filled zeppelins. The most spectacular of these airships, the *Hindenburg*, stretched the length of three football fields and regularly traveled across the Atlantic Ocean carrying passengers in style. And the show of size and strength did not end there. All over Germany, people gladly adopted Hitler's strict programs aimed at making the nation's young people well schooled, physically fit, and proud of their country.

"It all goes so fast," Owens said of the sprint races, "and character makes the difference when it's close."

57

Yet this glittering nation of fast highways and fit youngsters was being built at the expense of the livelihood and freedom of millions of its own people. Hitler's dream nation excluded anyone he did not consider a patriotic native of pure Aryan stock. And with fanatical and relentless energy he set about promoting a form of national pride that thrived on the oppression of anyone who did not fit that description.

When he had been in office just 1 month, Hitler ordered the creation of 50 concentration camps to imprison "enemies of the state." Four months later, 27,000 people—mostly Jews and Communists—were being held under brutal conditions in those camps. Soon, Catholics and members of other religious denominations were forced to join these prisoners in their misery, and thousands of others fled the country in fear.

Astute observers of the strange goings-on in Germany guessed what Hitler was up to. Those autobahns could be used to transport troops quickly and efficiently all over the country. Those zeppelins and the planes being turned out on German assembly lines could be fitted out for wartime purposes almost instantly. And all those schoolboys learning to toss balls accurately into hoops positioned on the ground might just as easily have been throwing grenades. Finally, if the Nazis saw fit to drive out or imprison a large part of their own population, who could say what they might do to other nations in a time of war?

But somehow, few people got the point. Maybe Hitler's clampdown on the German press was the reason. Maybe he charmed the world's leaders into trusting him. Maybe it was simply impossible to believe that a nation beaten into the ground in the ugliest war ever fought, scarcely 17 years earlier, could be thirsting for battle again so soon. Whatever the cause, Hitler began to carry out his plans for genocide

An awe-inspiring symbol of Germany's advanced technology, the zeppelin Hindenberg, the world's largest airship, navigates the skies of Nazi Germany in 1936.

and world domination with scarcely a whimper from other governments.

And in sponsoring the 1936 Olympic Games, he expected to pull off yet another coup, because here was his opportunity to hoodwink the people of the world, to perform a magnificent magician's trick directly under their noses. He invited the world's greatest athletes, the reporters with their radio hookups, the statesmen and socialites, right into his nation's capital and dared them to see anything but good.

But for Adolf Hitler, never one to pull his punches, merely sponsoring the Olympic Games was not enough. These sporting events supplied an ex-

Chancellor Adolf Hitler (above) and Owens (opposite) besieged by their respective fans in Germany. "I wanted no part of politics," Owens later said of the 1936 Games. "And I wasn't in Berlin to compete against any one athlete. The purpose of the Olympics, anyway, was to do your best. As I'd learned long ago from Charles Riley, the only victory that counts is the one over yourself."

cellent forum where his notions of Aryan supremacy might be tested. Germany had done well at the 1932 Games in Los Angeles, before Hitler's rise to power. The new chancellor had spared no expense to make sure the Germans would come out victorious this time.

Red-white-and-black Nazi swastika flags were flying from every shop window on June 24, when the U.S. Olympic team came down the S.S. *Manhattan*'s gangway in Bremerhaven, Germany, touching solid ground for the first time in a week. Catching an express train to Berlin, the team marveled at the beauty of the countryside. Berlin itself had been so carefully renovated for the Games that it seemed to sparkle.

The Germans had built a magnificent Olympic Village to house the athletes a few miles west of the city. This idea worked so well that similar villages have been built for every Olympics since then. The Berlin version included comfortable dormitories, a spacious park, a library, a swimming pool, and theaters. Owens roomed with his high school buddy and Ohio State teammate, high jumper David Albritten.

For two weeks, as other competitors arrived from around the world, the American track team worked off its "sea legs" at the practice track in the Olympic Village. Ohio State track coach Larry Snyder was not an official member of the U.S. delegation, but he had traveled to Berlin at his own expense to keep an eye on Owens and Albritten.

It was lucky for Owens that he did. One day, Snyder arrived at the track to find the Olympic coaches trying to change the running style that he, Coach Charles Riley, and Owens had all but perfected over the past several years. Those coaches were trying to alter Owens's effortless gliding run into the powerhouse style they favored, but Snyder stepped in to convince them to leave well enough alone.

Also, Owens had lost his track shoes at the Olympic Trials in New York, so Snyder spent days combing the shops of Berlin for a perfect replacement pair.

But there was nothing Snyder could do about all the autograph seekers and photographers who constantly surrounded his star. Adolf Hitler may have had a grudge against people from what he considered to be inferior races, but German youngsters were fascinated by the American who held all those world records. And Owens, always smiling and happy to oblige, won their hearts with the few German words he had picked up during his stay. He woke up every morning to the sight of curious faces pressed against his dormitory window, yet he handled the fishbowl of celebrity with a down-to-earth sense of humor that belied all the pressure of the upcoming Games.

By the time August 1 arrived, however, he and his teammates were eager to get on with the competition. They marched into the gigantic crater of a stadium to the roar of 100,000 fans and caught their first glimpse of the German chancellor. Hitler stood in uniform and at attention in his flag-draped viewing box, surrounded by his right-hand men: Hermann Goring, Albert Speer, and Joseph Goebbels—all names that would become notorious in the war years ahead.

Owens was largely unconcerned with all the pomp and politics. He had come to Berlin to run and jump. And the next day he got his chance. If he had any doubts about his physical condition after the voyage overseas, he quickly wiped them away in the 100-meter eliminations. Cold, drizzly rain fell most of the day, making the track slow and muddy. But without a word of complaint, Owens astounded the crowd by equaling his own world record of 10.3 seconds. In his afternoon heat, he lowered that time by a tenth of a second, but because of a following wind the new record was disallowed.

Reassured that he was still at the top of his form, Owens slipped on his sweat suit and spent the rest of the afternoon watching Albritten compete in the high jump. Before the day was over, both Albritten and his American teammate Cornelius Johnson had broken the world record in their event. Johnson squeezed out a victory with a remarkable leap of 2.3 meters (7 feet, 6¼ inches). Albritten, having hurt his ankle during the competition, admitted that he was pleased to have won the silver medal. He took it back to his dormitory room that night, where it did not remain alone for long.

The semifinals and finals of the 100-meter race were held the next day. As Owens warmed up for his semifinal heat, a cloudburst sent the spectators scurrying for cover and muddied the track even more. But this was the day Owens had lived for. The dream of a lifetime lay within his grasp.

Later, he would philosophize about the oddity of training so many years for an occasion that would be over in mere seconds. To the runner, he said, the race was both shorter and longer than a spectator could imagine: "To a sprinter, the hundred-yard dash is over in *three* seconds, not nine or ten. The first 'second' is when you come out of the blocks. The next is when you look up and take your first few strides to attain gain position. By that time the race is actually about half over. The final 'second'—the longest slice of time in the world for an athlete—is that last half of the race, when you really bear down and see what you're made of. It seems to take an eternity, yet is all over before you can think what's happening."

According to Owens, people assumed that running 100 meters was just a question of speed. Certainly, that was a lot of it. But against world-class

Owens (right) beating fellow American Ralph Metcalfe in the 100 meters to win the first of his Olympic gold medals. Owens's time of 10.3 seconds equaled the world mark.

One of Germany's most popular athletes, Luz Long (left), with his new friend Jesse Owens. To most people, their spirited competition in the long jump was the high point of the 1936 Olympic Games.

competition, the big challenge appeared in the last half of the race, when every instinct, all those years of training, and sheer courage were called upon to squeeze out every last drop of speed. This was what Coach Riley had been talking about in all his high school lectures when he said to "race against yourself." To go to the limit in this way was a supreme sporting achievement, and Jesse Owens carried it out so brilliantly that he made it look like child's play.

Owens won his semifinal heat easily, in 10.4 seconds. Then, in the 100-meter finals, he burst into the lead at the starting gun and was never challenged. He broke the tape in 10.3 seconds, tying his own Olympic record. Ralph Metcalfe, the Marquette University sprinter who had won two Olympic medals in Los Angeles, finished second, a yard back. But all eyes were on Owens. One British observer marveled, "No sprinter I have ever seen has run in such effortless style. He was in a class above all other competitors;

his arms and legs worked in perfect rhythm, and he carried his running right through the tape."

The results of the race were broadcast on loud-speakers all over Berlin, so, as Owens took his victory lap, shouts in and out of the stadium circled with him. The German crowd had found a hero in the college boy from the United States, and for the rest of the Games, wherever he went, the shout went up: "Yesseh Oh-vens! Yesseh Oh-vens!"

On the victory stand that afternoon, Owens's eyes misted over as he bent forward to receive his gold medal and watched the American flag being raised. He had achieved his dream at last. He would re-member this as the happiest moment of his whole career.

It was no such happy moment for Adolf Hitler. Owens bowed to him from the victory stand, and the German chancellor returned a stiff salute, then turned away. The Nazi leader had been working for years to build racial hatred in Germany, and here in just 10 seconds a black American had won the hearts of his countrymen. When an aide suggested that he invite Owens to his viewing box, Hitler savagely re-plied, "Do you really think that I will allow myself to be photographed shaking hands with a Negro?"

Whether Owens knew that he had been snubbed or not, he did not have time to be bothered by a racist politician. The next day, the preliminaries of the 200-meter race began. For the fourth day in a row, rain fell—this time as a bus drove the American track team to the stadium. Owens had to wear his sweatshirt to stay warm during his elimination heats, which he won handily. Then, while the other sprint-ers caught a bus back to the Olympic Village, he tried to stay loose for the afternoon's long-jump compe-tition, swallowing a damp sandwich for lunch.

The 100-meter victory had seemed so easy, but the long jump proved anything but. In fact, Owens barely made it into the finals. Each athlete was given three chances to qualify, which should have been two more than Owens needed. But when he ran, still wearing his sweat suit, through the long-jump pit to gauge the steps for his first leap, he was shocked to discover that the judges counted the run-through as his first attempt. Then, when he *did* jump, they said he had committed a foul by stepping over the takeoff board and disqualified the leap.

Now the pressure was on, and suddenly the power of concentration that had helped make Owens such a formidable competitor deserted him. In his autobiography, Owens recalled that this was the most frightening moment of his career: "I fought, fought hard, harder . . . but one cell at a time, panic crept into my body, taking me over."

He credited a German long jumper, Luz Long, with pulling him back together for his last leap. The German, who had already qualified for the finals, walked over and asked in his best English, "What has taken your goat, Jazze Owenz?" Owens had to smile at that.

The tension broken, Long suggested to Owens that in his third attempt he take his very last step several inches before the end of the takeoff board, thus making sure that he did not overstep the board and become disqualified. Owens thanked him for the advice, and with the old confidence returning, raced down the runway for his jump. Even though he leaped before the end of the takeoff board, where the officials begin their measurements, he landed more than 26 feet away, a new Olympic record. Again, Owens ran over to thank the German.

All afternoon, Owens and Long were locked in head-to-head competition for the long-jump gold medal. The Olympic record broke with each leap. Yet through it all they cheered each other on. The crowd had never seen anything like it. Long stood a few inches taller than Owens. He was the perfect picture of the Aryan superman—blond, blue eyed, with a perfectly proportioned physique. But he was not caught up in Hitler's mania for white supremacy. Like Owens, he understood that one competes primarily against oneself, and he seemed genuinely grateful to have at last met a man who could drive him on to a better performance.

Luz Long jumped with a simple, fluid style, his arms thrown high above his head. Owens "ran through" the jump, hitch kicking in midair as Coach Snyder had taught him, to capitalize on his superior speed. With each jump, the crowd erupted in applause. No doubt the Germans wanted their countryman to win, but Owens had already become a crowd favorite, and for once it was easy to join in the friendly spirit of competition that the two long jumpers shared.

In the final round, Long matched Owens's record. The two smiled and shook hands. Then Owens went to the board and jumped even further. More applause. Eventually, Long faltered, overrunning the board. A groan went up around the stadium. And with the gold medal awaiting him, Owens gathered himself for one more jump. With the regal confidence and concentration of a Babe Ruth, he sailed to a new Olympic record of 26 feet, 5⁵⁄₁₆ inches. Luz Long was the first to congratulate Owens, giving him a hearty bear hug in full view of Adolf Hitler.

That evening at the Olympic Village, Owens and Long were inseparable. Though Owens could not speak German and Long knew only a little English, they talked for hours. It turned out that Long had come from a poor family, too. Like Owens, he had a wife and child at home. They spoke about their love for their sport, which offered challenges nothing else could match, and fretted together over racial prejudice in Germany and the United States. By the

Luz Long makes his final leap in the 1936 Olympics long-jump competition. He was, according to Owens, "a supreme example of Aryan perfection . . . one of those rare athletic happenings you come to recognize after years in competition—a perfectly proportioned body, every lithe but powerful cord a celebration of pulsing natural muscle, stunningly compressed and honed by tens of thousands of obvious hours of sweat and determination. He may have been my archenemy, but I had to stand there in awe and just stare at Luz Long for several seconds."

"I decided I wasn't going to come down," Owens said of his final leap in the long-jump competition. "I was going to fly. I was going to stay up in the air forever." He won the Olympic event with a record leap of 26 feet, 5⁵/₁₆ inches.

time the Olympic Games ended, the two had become firm friends. And as their relationship was portrayed in newspapers worldwide, they came to represent the way supposed archenemies can overcome their differences. Beyond all of Hitler's flag-waving and speeches, the image of Jesse Owens and Luz Long shaking hands became the overriding symbol of the 1936 Olympics.

Owens awoke the next day to more rain. He breezed through his semifinal heat in the 200 meters, then spent the afternoon watching Americans Ken Carpenter and Earle Meadows win gold medals in the discus and pole vault, respectively. Then, just before sunset, in the 200-meter finals, Owens again proved himself the world's fastest human. On top of all his tutoring by Coaches Riley and Snyder, he had developed a trick or two of his own over the years. One of these accounted in part for his quick takeoffs at the starting gun. Out of the corner of his eye he watched the starter, knowing that there was usually some telltale sign just as the trigger was pulled, and that sign gave Owens a slight jump on his competitors. This technique worked well in Berlin, where the starter habitually bobbed his knees just before pulling the trigger.

Owens knew he would need all his skill to win the 200-meter race. After he had set a new Olympic record of 21.1 seconds in his preliminary heat, teammate Mack Robinson equaled that mark later in the morning. Yet Robinson could not keep up with Owens in the final. Owens held a slight lead coming out of the turn, and when he reached the tape Robinson trailed him by nearly five yards. Owens's time of 20.7 seconds set a new world record for a 200-meter race around a curve. But the crowd had barely finished shouting its approval when the skies opened again. Owens received his third gold medal during a downpour.

At last, the competition had ended for him. He could spend the remaining days in Berlin rooting for his American teammates, enjoying performances by circus animals, dance troupes, and even the Berlin Philharmonic at the Olympic Village, or trying to make out the shadowy images of other athletes on a prototype television set.

Then the U.S. coaches called him to a meeting. They believed the Germans were saving their best runners for the 400-meter relay race, and for that reason they wanted Owens to run the first leg for the American team. Ralph Metcalfe would run the second leg, virtually assuring an American victory in the event. It is not difficult to imagine the anger of

Owens (right) in a 200-meter heat, setting an Olympic record for the distance with a time of 21.1 seconds. In the finals, he bettered the mark by an extraordinary amount, four-tenths of a second, to win his third gold medal. Mack Robinson, an older brother of baseball great Jackie Robinson, captured the silver medal.

sprinters Marty Glickman and Sam Stoller, who had been slated to run the relay, when they were told that they were being bumped from the race. Owens also seemed surprised. He told the coaches he had enough gold medals and to let the others run.

But the coaches would not budge. Glickman and Stoller, the only Jewish members of the U.S. Olympic team, thus became the only two team members who did not compete at the Games. And by making the change, U.S. officials seemed suspiciously close to the racist notions that fueled the Nazi government. Their decision made it plain to all that anti-Semitism was not simply a German problem.

When race day came, Owens, of course, did his best. He handed the baton to Metcalfe with a five-yard lead. Foy Draper started his leg ahead by 7 yards, and Frank Wykoff, who took the baton 10 yards in the lead, lengthened it to 12 by the end of the race. The Americans set a new world record of 39.8 seconds. The Italians won the silver medal, and the Germans came in third. The rumor of a German superteam had amounted to nothing.

Jesse Owens had won his fourth gold medal, an unprecedented feat by a track athlete. He had broken Olympic records in all four events. This achievement overreached his wildest dreams and made him a hero to sports fans worldwide.

One of those fans proved to be Hitler's hand-picked cinematographer, Leni Riefenstahl. She filmed the entire 1936 Olympic Games in a sweeping, lyrical style that highlighted the beauty of each event

Owens competing in the 400-meter relay, on his way to his fourth Olympic gold medal, a record number for a track-and-field athlete.

Wearing the victor's laurels, Owens salutes the American flag during an Olympic medal ceremony. "It dawned on me with blinding brightness," he later said of his Olympic achievements. "I realized: I had jumped into another rare kind of stratosphere—one that only a handful of people in every generation are lucky enough to know."

while downplaying all the hoopla over winners and losers. Jesse Owens was her athletic ideal. In her filming of the 100-meter competition, her cameraman zoomed in on Owens's thigh, neglecting all the other runners to show his perfectly toned muscles in action.

Similarly, her portrayal of the Owens-Long duel in the long jump centers on the soaring grace of their leaps, not on their battle for the gold. Riefenstahl's film, *Olympiad*, is sometimes shown on television, especially during Olympic years, and it is easy for a viewer to be drawn into her awe at the magnificence of athletic achievement and particularly at the seem-ingly effortless beauty of Jesse Owens in full flight.

As the Americans packed their bags at the Olym-pic Village, they already looked forward to the next Games. These were to be held in Tokyo, Japan, in 1940, when Owens would be just 26 years old. Cer-tainly, he would be back to compete again.

But the Germans and the Japanese had goals other than sports in mind. A wooden peg in the closet of each dormitory room had been placed there to hold a helmet. Already in the fields near the Olympic Village machine-gun practice could be heard. The village would become an infantry training center as soon as the athletes departed.

World War II would put an end to any talk of a 1940 or a 1944 Olympics. The German swastika flag would become a hated emblem to people all over the world. As Owens carefully packed his four gold med-als for the trip home, he could not have known that he would never compete at another Olympics. And he would never again see his new friend Luz Long either. Like Owens's relay-race teammate Foy Draper, Long would die in a foxhole during the war. ❧

6

AFTER
THE
GOLD RUSH

W HAT DOES A 22 year old do when he has
achieved his wildest dream? As the possibilities piled
up following his Olympic victories, Jesse Owens could
not have guessed that this question would torment
him for the rest of his life. It had been one thing to
aim his formidable talents at the single goal repre-
sented by those five interlocked Olympic hoops. Test-
ing himself against the constantly shifting demands
of the workaday world would prove a far more difficult
challenge.

Coach Larry Snyder wasted no time in coming to
Owens's aid. He arrived in the athlete's room the
evening following the 400-meter relay race for a private, man-to-man talk. He had not come to discuss
race strategy or running form—none of that mattered
anymore—but to consider how Owens might best
capitalize on his Olympian achievements. At that
moment, it seemed there were two options: return to
Ohio State to complete his degree or drop out of
school to make some money from his newfound celebrity.

Even though Owens was the unparalleled star of
the school's track team, Coach Snyder was a practical
man, and he knew that offers would soon come pouring in proposing huge amounts for Owens's services.
As the Olympic star told a reporter the next morning,
"I'm anxious to finish my college career, but I can't

*The conquering hero: Owens dis-
plays the three gold medals that he
won for his individual prowess in
the 1936 Olympics.*

A hero's welcome: Owens is greeted by his mother and wife (above) in New York City and is cheered by his hometown fans in Cleveland (opposite, at back of lead car) shortly after returning from the 1936 Olympics in Berlin. "You worked—possibly slaved is the word—Jesse, for many years for this," his wife told him. "And you deserve everything they're saying about you and doing for you."

afford to miss this chance if it really means big money. I can always go back and get a degree."

Even before Owens had his bags packed, the offers began to arrive. A California orchestra wired him that it would pay him $25,000 just for introducing songs onstage for 2 weeks. Entertainer Eddie Cantor wanted to share a vaudeville stage with Owens, proposing a $40,000 fee for 10 weeks of work. And Paramount Pictures talked of a movie deal.

All those zeros made the runner's head spin. To a depression-era American, the sums seemed astronomical. All Owens wanted to do was get home, show those medals to his family, and rest a while before sorting out the opportunities.

But the AAU and the U.S. Olympic Committee had other plans. In order to pay team expenses, they had set up post-Olympic track meets all over Europe, and Owens was to be their star gate attraction. Exhausted from a week of record-breaking performances, he had to join his teammates on a trip to Dresden, then on to Cologne and Prague, and back to Bochum, Germany, staging track-and-field exhibitions at each stop. Not surprisingly, the team performed unevenly. If Owens equaled his world record in the 100-meter dash in one city, he lost out to an unknown athlete in the long jump elsewhere.

By the time the team boarded a plane for London, they were homesick, dog tired, and flat broke. Coach Snyder, angry at the shoddy treatment the AAU was showing some of the world's best athletes, called a stop to it right there. After a meeting with university officials, he announced that Owens was simply too tired to go on. He would run one last time in London and then board a ship for New York.

At the London meet, the American team trounced all comers. Owens, however, competed only on the 400-meter relay team. The 90,000 spectators who had come to see the Olympic stars perform could

not have known that they were witnessing the last amateur race Owens would ever run.

But thanks to the arrogance of AAU officials, that is what happened. Avery Brundage and the other businessmen who ran the U.S. Olympic team were not about to lose their star athlete in the midst of such a lucrative tour—at least not without a fight. They told Snyder to make sure Owens caught the plane to the next meet in Stockholm, or else. When Owens failed to board that plane, the outraged officials suspended him indefinitely from amateur competition. Never mind that the entire world knew about his exploits a week earlier on the track in Berlin. Never mind that he was a hero to people everywhere. Once again, the AAU proved its stubborn

"Don't do anything till you see me!" Bill "Bojangles" Robinson (right), one of America's best-known black entertainers, told Owens by ship-to-shore telephone as the Olympic champion made his way back to the United States in August 1936 aboard the Queen Mary. Robinson arranged for his manager to handle the business offers that came Owens's way.

narrow-mindedness, punishing its greatest athlete simply for wanting to go home.

At least the suspension freed Owens to do what he wanted: He caught the next ship back to the States. Aboard the *Queen Mary* he relaxed, danced, and regained the 10 pounds he had lost during the stress of the Olympics. By the time he arrived in New York four days later, he felt rejuvenated and ready to face the hero's welcome awaiting him.

And what a hero's welcome it was. Owens's family was brought out on a launch to meet the ship even before it docked in New York harbor. The women smothered him with kisses. Then, at the dock, Owens answered the questions of clamoring reporters until the great entertainer Bill "Bojangles" Robinson rescued him and his family for a fast-moving motorcade to Harlem. At Robinson's home, Owens found himself the guest of honor of the city's black luminaries, who seemed as eager to shake his hand as the German schoolchildren had been.

Finally, when the party died down, Robinson took Owens aside and introduced the athlete to his show-business agent, Marty Forkins. The agent and the performer had taken sprinter Eddie Tolan under their wing following his victory at the Los Angeles Olympics, and they said they would now be happy to guide Owens through the strange waters of celebrity. His mind spinning with their talk of a Hollywood fortune, Owens gathered his family to catch a train back to Cleveland and the well-deserved rest he had dreamed of ever since he left Berlin.

But Owens's hometown fans could not let him rest without first getting a glimpse of their hero. A motorcade wound its way through Cleveland's East Side ghetto and through the fanciest streets in town on its way to welcoming speeches at City Hall. Then it was on to Columbus for another victory procession and more speeches. Finally, three weeks after leaving the Olympics, Owens got a chance to sleep in his own bed.

But he was up the next day to haggle with Coach Snyder and Ohio State administrators over what he would do next. Everyone agreed that his best bet at cashing in on his fame was to sign an agency agreement with Forkins. He could always get his college degree later.

So Owens climbed back on the train for New York. While in Manhattan, he met his Olympic teammates as they arrived from Europe, and he rode in the first car of the ticker-tape parade up Broadway that honored their return. Once again, Bill "Bojangles" Robinson was waiting for him. At the final

Owens with his wife at the Cotton Club in Harlem. Following the 1936 Olympics, a number of deals and endorsements for Owens were arranged at the nightclub.

ceremony, held on nearby Randall's Island that afternoon, Owens showed his gratitude to his new friend by giving him one of the gold medals he had won in Berlin.

With all the victory parades out of the way, Owens sat back and waited to pick his way through the many job offers he had received. Then, one by one, before his eyes, they all disappeared. Eddie Cantor backed out of his promise to take Owens on tour, as did the California orchestra that had sounded so eager in Berlin. All the talk of movie deals faded away, too. As Owens remembered years later, "After I came home from the 1936 Olympics with my four medals, it became increasingly apparent that everyone was going to slap me on the back, want to shake my hand or have me up to their suite. But no one was going to offer me a job."

Owens (right) stumping for Republican presidential candidate Alf Landon (opposite, center) in the fall of 1936. An exceptional public speaker, Owens "doesn't so much take [a room] over as envelop it," said one reporter. "He is friendly to all, outgoing and gracious."

To make matters worse, the Olympic champion could not compete in track meets anymore. Signing an agency contract had been the last straw for the AAU. Already angry over Owens's dropping out of the European tour, the organization said that he was now a professional and was therefore ineligible to compete as an amateur ever again.

What was Owens to do now? He did the one thing he knew how to do best: He ran. But this time he was running from a banquet to a radio broadcast to a clothing or food endorsement and back to another banquet, earning $1,000 or so at each stop. Any offer Forkins dug up, Owens took. In the months following his return from Berlin, Owens traveled all over the United States, trading his fame for whatever money he could make. No single job amounted to much, but all together they added up to a small fortune.

Before the year was out, Owens had bought his parents a big house, his wife an expensive wardrobe and jewelry, and himself a spanking new Buick sedan. He even took Charles Riley to an auto showroom, trading in that old Model T for a new Chevy.

When the Republican party asked Owens to campaign for its presidential candidate, Alf Landon, Owens balked at first, saying he did not care much about politics. But when they reminded him that President Franklin D. Roosevelt, the Democratic candidate in the 1936 presidential race, had not even sent a telegram of congratulations following his Olympic victories, Owens changed his mind. Now he was running the political race, too. At whistle-stops all over America, Owens used the speech-making skills he had learned at Ohio State, telling charming anecdotes about his experiences in Berlin and ending each talk with a few words in support of Landon. For this, he earned somewhere between $10,000 and $15,000. All of Owens's public-speaking

In late 1936, Owens's business manager, Marty Forkins (left), arranged for his client to race in Cuba against the country's fastest athlete, Conrado Rodriques. The staging of the race was sabotaged by the Amateur Athletic Union, however, which regarded Owens as a professional and threatened Rodriques with the loss of his amateur status if he took part in the contest.

skills could not help Landon, however. He lost to Roosevelt in a landslide, carrying only two states, Vermont and Maine.

Owens was determined to make a living no matter how he had to do it, and he poured all of his athletic intensity into the project. If no one wanted to hire a black Olympic champion, then he would get along as well as he could. When Forkins offered him the opportunity to race in Cuba on the day after Christmas, 1936, Owens reluctantly agreed to pass up the holiday at home. The race was supposed to be against Cuba's fastest sprinter, Conrado Rodriques. But the AAU, watching every move Owens made, warned Rodriques that by racing against a professional he risked his own amateur standing.

Owens arrived in Havana on Christmas Day only to learn that the race would not go off as scheduled. The fast-talking promoter, however, said he had something else in mind that might work. He asked if Owens would be willing to run against a horse. At first, Owens must have thought this was a joke. Did the promoter know that he had learned to run from watching horses race? What was he to do? He was in Cuba at Christmas, the money was on the table: Why not?

The race took place at halftime of a soccer game. To make matters worse, when Owens jogged onto the field rain came pouring down. Only 3,000 fans remained in the stands. And there at the starting line was his competition, jockey J. M. Contino, astride the thoroughbred Julio McCaw. Owens later said that he felt sick at that moment, realizing what he was about to do. But he went through with it. He lined up with a 40-yard head start and raced 100 yards further down the field, beating the horse by several steps. Then he took the $2,000 payment and went home.

When Owens's match race with Cuban sprinter Conrado Rodriques was canceled, business agent Marty Forkins (far right) arranged for Owens to run against the thoroughbred Julio McCaw. "It was bad enough to have toppled from the Olympic heights to make my living competing with animals," Jesse said. "But the competition wasn't even fair. No man could beat a race horse, not even for 100 yards."

It did not escape Owens's notice how far he had fallen in just four months since the Olympic Games. He was at that moment one of the most famous people in the world, and newspapers everywhere carried photographs of his race against the horse. Some even quoted Owens, saying how good it felt to be out running again. But if fans were dismayed at their hero's misfortune, Owens had never been one to complain. And if racing against horses or campaigning for a politician would help support his family, he would do it again.

This is how, in the weeks following his Olympic triumph, Jesse Owens set the stage for the rest of his life. ❧

7

BARNSTORMIN'

THE ONLY PERSON who came through on his promise to help Jesse Owens after the 1936 Olympics was Bill "Bojangles" Robinson. The veteran showman fitted the runner out in a white suit and tails, briefed him on holding the attention of a nightclub audience, and helped him win a whopping $100,000 contract to lead a 12-piece black touring band. Ruth Owens was now expecting her second child. She had just picked out a new house in Cleveland and was busy decorating. But she would have to make that house a home by herself, because in January 1937 her famous husband hit the road.

Years later, Owens would laugh while describing to William O. Johnson, Jr., author of *All That Glitters Is Not Gold: The Olympic Games*, his months as a bandleader: "Well, I couldn't play an instrument. I'd just stand up front and announce the numbers. They had me sing a little, but that was a horrible mistake. I can't carry a tune in a bucket. We played black theaters and nightclubs all over hell. One-nighters. Apollo Theater in Harlem and the Earle Theater in Philly—that was big time for blacks."

In January 1937, Consolidated Radio Artists sought to capitalize on Owens's fame by offering him the position of bandleader of a 12-piece orchestra. The music company reportedly paid him $100,000, making it one of the most lucrative deals Owens ever made.

Sometimes, Owens would scout out the town he awoke in, and if a baseball game was scheduled there, he would cut a deal for a running exhibition between innings. It was a grueling life, fights often broke out on the dance floors, and Owens missed his family. Finally, he came down with strep throat in Richmond, Virginia, and called it quits, giving up that huge contract for a chance at some home cooking and more than a glimpse of his baby daughter, Marlene.

At that time, freewheeling basketball teams toured the country, dazzling the locals with their prowess. Today, the Harlem Globetrotters are the last of these teams to survive, but in the fall of 1937, when Owens formed a team of Cleveland hotshots he named the Olympians, there were similar groups all over. Owens went out on the road with this crew, which played in large and small towns across America. Before spring came, the Olympians had played 142 games, winning all but 6. As an added attraction, Owens often ran exhibition races at halftime. But when the season ended, the team had barely broken even, and Owens returned home looking for new money-making ventures.

He hired some of the same players for a barnstorming softball team called the Olympics and traveled with them on weekends in the summer. But by now he was finding it difficult to pay his debts, especially the notes on his and his parents' new homes. Coach Riley discovered to his dismay that Owens had covered only the down payment on his Chevy, and Riley had to struggle on his teacher's salary to make the monthly payments.

So Owens decided to get a job. At just over $1,000 for the summer, his position as a bathhouse attendant for Cleveland's recreation department was a far cry from his stipend as a bandleader, but at least it helped pay the bills. Before the summer ended, he

had parlayed that job into a better-paying position as a playground director.

But those legs that had run so far were not ready to quit yet. For the grand opening of nighttime baseball at Ebbetts Field in Brooklyn, New York, Owens showed up to race against the fastest athletes baseball had to offer. At another game in Chicago later that summer, he challenged heavyweight boxing champion Joe Louis to a 60-yard sprint.

And Owens raced against horses, too, learning after a while a few circus tricks to make it easier. As he told William O. Johnson, Jr., "The secret is, first, get a thoroughbred horse because they are the most nervous animals on earth. Then get the biggest gun you can find and make sure the starter fires that big

The Olympians, a basketball team founded by Owens (front row) in the fall of 1937, competed against amateur squads, semiprofessional clubs, and college teams. At halftime of each game, Owens spoke to the crowd and demonstrated his running techniques. On occasion, he also took part in an exhibition race.

Owens races against two of major-league baseball's fastest players, Ernie Koy (left) and Lee Gamble (center), before the start of the first night game ever played at Ebbetts Field in Brooklyn, New York. Owens was narrowly defeated in the 100-yard dash after giving the ballplayers a 10-yard head start.

gun right by that nervous thoroughbred's ear." By the time the jockey got his mount settled down, Owens would be halfway down the track. Still, the races were close.

For Owens, it would never be enough just to hold a job, run a baseball team, and tour as a runner-for-hire. Before long, he had started a dry-cleaning business as well. The first of these establishments opened on Cleveland's East Side, where Owens had grown up. The sign out front read, Speedy 7-Hour Service by the World's Fastest Human. Constantly on the road, Owens left the dry cleaning to business partners and signed on to tour for a while with a team of baseball-playing comedians aptly named the Indianapolis Clowns.

Owens had never been much of a ballplayer, however. He later said that his role came at the end of the game, as the grand finale: "We'd get into these little towns and tell 'em to get out the fastest guy in town and Jesse Owens'd spot him ten yards and beat him." This is why there are old men all over America still telling yarns about racing against Jesse Owens. Many of them actually did.

But maintaining all of these ventures at the same time eventually proved too much for Owens. All at once, the whole world seemed to come crashing down. It started when the Internal Revenue Service demanded payment for back taxes. Owens lost the dry-cleaning business trying to pay that debt. Then, in March 1940, his beloved mother, Mary Emma, his first and greatest inspiration, died at the age of 64. In a car crash that summer, Owens's Buick was totally destroyed. He escaped with a few bruises, but the brush with death was terrifying. As a final blow, his world record in the 220-yard low hurdles fell, another sign of his mortality. When his third daughter, Beverly, was born, Owens realized it was time to take stock of where he was headed.

Owens made the courageous choice to start from scratch. In the fall of 1940, he returned to Ohio State to get his degree. Even though the AAU still refused to allow him to compete as an amateur, Coach Larry Snyder gladly hired him to help with the track team. Owens's entire family moved to Columbus, and he settled into the life of a student.

Yet as hard as he tried, the 27-year-old college junior could not make it work. In September, his father died of a heart attack. Owens mourned while sweating over the tough required courses he had postponed during his glory years. Finally, he had to face the fact that he would never get a diploma. In December 1941, halfway through his second year back in school, he called it quits. His average on a 4.0 scale was just 1.07.

That same month, the Japanese bombed the Pearl Harbor naval base in Hawaii, and the United States entered World War II. Because he was the head of a household, Owens was not drafted into military service, but the government nevertheless found a role for him at home. The Civilian Defense Office put Owens in charge of a national physical fitness orga-

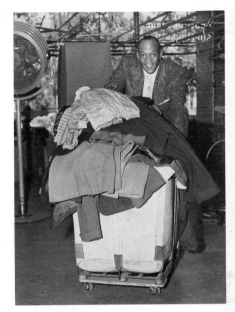

The Cleveland-based Jesse Owens Dry Cleaning Company, established in the summer of 1938, was a business opportunity that Owens said he "grabbed . . . like you grab the baton in a relay race from a man who's almost out of the legal passing zone—just in time." The venture struggled from the start, however, and collapsed less than a year later.

In the fall of 1940, Owens (left) returned to Ohio State with the hope of earning his college degree. He helped pay for his tuition by assisting Larry Snyder as coach of the track team.

nization. For a year, he toured the country setting up exercise programs at black schools and community halls.

Then Owens was offered the best job he would ever hold. Ford Motor Company, which was turning its assembly lines into military factories for the war effort, hired him as a personnel officer for its thousands of black workers in Detroit. This was the perfect job for a man with limitless energy, prestige, and a way of getting along with almost anybody.

Owens started out by mediating difficulties that came up between the company and the United Auto Workers of America union. But by the time the war ended, Owens had expanded his position so that he was helping black workers find better housing, establishing recreation facilities in their neighborhoods, and welcoming new immigrants to the Motor City. At last, he had found work that allowed him to use his talents in a way that not only paid his rent but helped others as well. Not since he had thrilled the crowds at the Olympics had he felt this good.

But when the Germans, and then the Japanese, surrendered in 1945, Owens had to surrender his job as well. With Ford restructuring itself to make cars again, many of the wartime managers, including Owens, were dismissed.

He went back to his old barnstorming ways, touring for a while with the Harlem Globetrotters. At an exhibition in Milwaukee in 1950, at the age of 37, he ran a 100-yard dash in the astounding time of 9.7 seconds, less than half a second off his own world record. One wonders what feats he might have accomplished had the Olympic Games been held during the interim. But he could not go on like that forever. And besides, he had caught a glimpse of another way of life during his years at Ford. Jesse Owens would never be one to stay put for long, but in his remaining

During World War II, the Civilian Defense Office made Owens coordinator of a nationwide physical fitness program. Federal government officials also asked him to supervise the hiring of black workers at Detroit's Ford Motor Company plant, which was serving as a military factory during the war.

Owens, at the age of 34, outruns a 7-year-old pacer, The Ocean, in a 100-yard dash. Pointing out that he "worked as few men ever have," Owens continued to appear in racing exhibitions well into the 1950s.

years he would find a way to combine his need to constantly keep moving with the opportunity to make more money than he had ever imagined earning.

The key was public relations. As American companies grew larger and more powerful in the years after World War II, they spent more money on advertising and on making themselves look good to their customers. Olympic hero Jesse Owens, the first American to put Hitler in his place, seemed the perfect choice to promote their goods.

Today, of course, when athletes and rock stars advertise all sorts of products at every opportunity, public relations of this sort is commonplace. But at that time, during the infancy of television, companies were just beginning to recognize the advantages of having a celebrity sell their wares.

Owens became the self-admitted prototype of the "famous flack." In Chicago, where he moved his family in 1949, he held public relations positions for clothing factories, insurance companies, and dry cleaners while plugging a variety of other products on television and radio. He was so swamped with offers that he had to form his own public relations firm to keep track of them all. Fourteen years after his Olympic triumph, some of the reward for his toil in Berlin had begun to come through.

But as he recalled in his autobiography, it all just meant more work: "People who worked with me or knew me still called me the 'world's fastest human' because I almost never stopped. I'd found that I could get more done with no regular job or regular hours at all, but by being on my own, flying to speak here, help with a public relations campaign for some client there, tape my regular jazz radio show one morning at 5:00 A.M. before leaving on a plane for another city or another continent three hours later to preside over a major sporting event."

Owens's barnstorming days were over. Never again would he have to race against a horse or some cocky local yokel to make ends meet. From the pinnacle of success at the Berlin Olympics, he had fallen very far. But each year, until the day he died, his Olympic gold medals would shine brighter. ❧

8

A PATCHWORK QUILT

JESSE OWENS'S SECOND wave of fame began in 1950, when the Associated Press named him the greatest track-and-field athlete in history. He was given the award at a huge banquet in Chicago, where he then lived, attended by 600 business leaders and sportsmen. Owens's acceptance speech sounded a lot like the other speeches he had been giving for years. He reminisced about his rough childhood, used his memory of German long jumper Luz Long to demonstrate how even enemies can overcome their differences, and swore by the difficult lesson he had learned over the past several years—that with hard work, even a poor boy can make good in America.

This was exactly what the business leaders wanted to hear. These were the years of the cold war with the Soviet Union, when Communism became a dirty word in the United States and many people were hounded from their jobs for not seeming patriotic enough. Almost overnight, Jesse Owens became a symbol of the "American way of life." It was not that he was saying anything differently than he ever had before; it was just that now those words readily blended in with the mood of the country. A registered

Owens acting as an American goodwill ambassador, on a tour of India, Malaysia, and the Philippines in 1955. The U.S. State Department asked him to visit the Far East to foster international friendship.

Republican ever since his ill-fated campaign for Alf Landon in 1936, Owens soon became a favorite of Republican president Dwight D. Eisenhower.

While corporations scrambled to get Owens to endorse their products, the president sent him overseas as a goodwill representative of the government. On one of these tours, when he traveled through Berlin, he met the son of his long-lost friend Luz Long. It was the youngster who broke the news to Owens that Long had been killed in the trenches during the war. Just as he had done with the high jumper years before, Owens talked with the young man late into the night.

Back in Chicago, Owens joined the board of directors of the South Side Boys Club, where he personally organized programs to help out troubled youngsters in the city's black ghetto. Appointed chairman of the Illinois State Athletic Commission, he worked hard to promote sport as a way out of poverty for poor youngsters. Meanwhile, he kept up his usual schedule of publicity appearances and radio shows, somehow finding time to tour the Far East as a goodwill ambassador for the State Department. This was a backbreaking schedule, and it would only accelerate in the years ahead.

But gradually, as Owens raced from airport to airport, he began to tire of it all. He wrote, "I was getting to be just another old jockstrap. . . . Maybe I was fur-lined, but I was still a jockstrap." When his long-standing world records in the 100-yard dash and 400-meter relay fell, that feeling hit him harder. Jesse Owens was 43 years old now. His daughter Marlene had just enrolled at his alma mater, Ohio State University. Yet he had to admit to himself that he still had not found anything to compare with the youthful thrill of those Olympic Games so long ago.

He never would. One by one, his world records fell, the last being his long-jump mark, which Amer-

ican Ralph Boston overtook at the 1960 Olympics in Rome. Interviewed there about his feelings, Owens shrugged and said, "It's like having a pet dog for a long time. You get attached to it, and when it dies you miss it."

That same year, Owens had the haunting experience of appearing on "This Is Your Life," a television show in which celebrity guests won the mixed blessing of being surprised by faces from their past. Coach Charles Riley, old and feeble by now, made the trip from his retirement home in Sarasota, Florida, to Los Angeles for the show. It dawned on Owens that he had not taken the time to see his old mentor in 15 years. And this was the last time the two would meet. Riley died a few months later.

Owens was aware, too, that he hardly knew his family. All three of his daughters were grown and gone. His wife, Ruth, had done what she could to make a good family life for them all, but like the constant world traveler that he had become, Owens realized that his family existed for him primarily as

Owens at a swimming class in Chicago. In the mid-1950s, he received two government appointments to which he was particularly well suited: secretary of the Illinois State Athletic Commission and executive director of the Juvenile Delinquency Prevention Program for the Illinois State Youth Commission. Both jobs required that Owens travel all over the state, organizing and supervising sports activities.

snapshots in his wallet. Yet he could not stop himself. The constant running had begun to seem like a tread-mill that he could not get off.

Owens campaigned for Richard Nixon in 1960 in a losing presidential battle against John F. Kennedy, and in 1965 he joined the hapless New York Mets at their training camp as a running coach. Even a rup-tured disc suffered while with the Mets, and the re-sulting neurosurgery, did not slow him down for long. Meanwhile, the list of products he endorsed grew and grew. His corporate clients included Ford Motor Company, Sears Roebuck, Atlantic-Richfield, and U.S. Rubber. During the 1968 Olympics, he ap-peared in television advertisements for Schlitz beer.

It was at those 1968 Olympic Games, held in Mexico City, that this self-professed "old jockstrap" really began to feel the pinch of age. As usual, he

Still on the run: Owens shows he remains in excellent form 25 years after his world-record-breaking performances at the Big Ten Championships.

arrived at the Games only to be mobbed by throngs of adoring fans. But as a paid consultant to the U.S. Olympic Committee, he had serious work to do. Nineteen sixty-eight was a year of revolt and upheaval around the world. The civil rights movement and opposition to the Vietnam War raged in the United States, and just one week before the Olympics began hundreds of student demonstrators had been shot by police in Mexico City. To a conservative Republican like Jesse Owens, things seemed out of control.

The great American sprinters that year were Tommie Smith and John Carlos, both students at San Jose State University in California. Tall and powerful, Smith had held 11 world records, and he blazed to a new 200-meter mark of 19.8 seconds in the Olympic final. Carlos won the bronze, finishing less than a step behind. They arrived at the podium to receive their medals barefoot. This was intended as a remembrance of black poverty in the United States. As the American flag rose, they raised their right fists encased in black gloves—a black power salute—and bowed their heads.

This gesture was an elegant example of nonviolent protest, but beamed worldwide by satellite television, it set off a wave of indignation in conservative circles. Jesse Owens, the man whose performance in Berlin had itself seemed a protest against Hitler's racism, was called in to help. He sat down with Smith and Carlos afterward, begging them to apologize. He told them, "The black fist is a meaningless symbol. When you open it, you have nothing but fingers— weak, empty fingers. The only time the black fist has significance is when there's money inside. There's where the power lies." Smith and Carlos looked at this man who had been their hero and realized that more than a generation gap lay between them. They refused to apologize and were promptly kicked off the U.S. Olympic team.

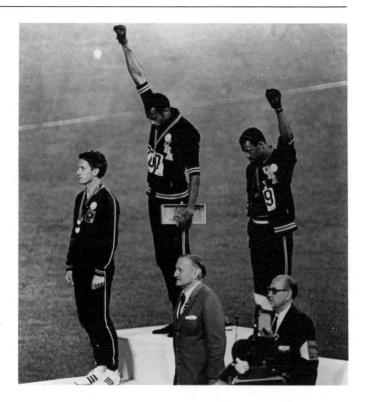

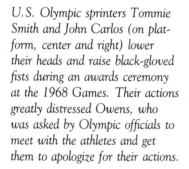

U.S. Olympic sprinters Tommie Smith and John Carlos (on platform, center and right) lower their heads and raise black-gloved fists during an awards ceremony at the 1968 Games. Their actions greatly distressed Owens, who was asked by Olympic officials to meet with the athletes and get them to apologize for their actions.

Owens went home furious. Somehow, he failed to make the connection between their performance in Mexico City and his own in Berlin. With sportswriter Paul Neimarck, he dashed off a book entitled *Blackthink: My Life as Black Man and White Man*, determined to show the world that not all black Americans were militants.

Blackthink, which was published in 1970, is a strange book, filled with a middle-aged man's anger and confusion at a changing world. In it, Owens lashes out at the nation's civil rights leaders, calling them complainers and "pro-Negro bigots." Those civil rights leaders found it hard to forgive Owens for his accusations, particularly this line: "If the Negro doesn't succeed in today's America, it is because he has chosen to fail."

Though the mainstream press supported *Blackthink*, angry letters poured into Owens's Chicago home. His barber refused to cut Owens's hair after reading the book. One reader suggested Owens take another look at the nation he had been racing across for 30 years, including with his letter a copy of the angry autobiography *Soul on Ice* by black militant Eldridge Cleaver. Bewildered by the stir he had caused, Owens sat down and read the book. It opened his eyes to the prejudice and hard times faced by many black Americans, difficulties that, because of his fame, he had been able to skirt most of his life.

So Owens wrote a new book, *I Have Changed*. Published in 1972, it is his apology for the bullheaded arrogance of *Blackthink*. "I realized now," he wrote, "that militancy in the *best* sense of the word was the *only* answer where the black man was concerned, that any black man who wasn't a militant in 1970 was either blind or a coward."

Owens added, however, that for him militancy did not mean violence, unless violence meant survival. He wanted to carve out a middle ground between conservatives and the youthful militants. He called it the "immoderate moderate." Like many Americans of his generation at that time, Owens had been shaken by the events of the 1960s and came out on the other side changed.

Changed, but not slowed down. Writer William O. Johnson, Jr., caught up with him on a speaking tour in 1971 and saw Owens in full stride: "He is a kind of all-around super-combination of nineteenth-century spellbinder and twentieth-century plastic P.R. man, a full-time banquet guest, eternal glad-hander and evangelistic small-talker. Muted, tasteful, inspirational bombast is his stock in trade."

Owens himself might not have argued with Johnson. In *I Have Changed*, he marveled at the half million miles he traveled each year, listing the events of one average week: "In the space of less than seven days, I attended a track meet in Boston, flew from there to Bowling Green for the National Jaycees, then to Rochester for the blind, Buffalo for another track meet, New York to shoot a film called, 'The Black Athlete,' Miami for Ford Motor Company, back up to New York for 45 minutes to deliver a speech, then into L.A. for another the same night."

For years, Ruth had pleaded with her prosperous husband to slow down and enjoy the wealth he had earned. At last, he agreed to move from the hustle and bustle of Chicago to quieter Scottsdale, Arizona. He was 65 years old now, the age when most workers retire. Yet he could not give up the road for the golf links and rarely made it home.

But the great athlete's health gradually began to fail. That winter, he caught pneumonia—the illness that had haunted his childhood. Then, during a speech in St. Louis, Missouri, a few days after Thanksgiving, 1979, Owens had to suddenly leave the stage. He went to see his doctor in Chicago only to hear two terrifying words: lung cancer. Owens had smoked cigarettes for 30 years, and at last the habit had taxed his mighty lungs past their limit.

The doctors treated Owens all winter, only to see him grow weaker. Still, they often caught him on the telephone, lobbying President Jimmy Carter and American athletic officials in an effort to keep them from boycotting the 1980 Olympic Games, which were to be held in Moscow. He lost out in that effort. American athletes did not compete in the 1980 Olympics. But he did not live to hear that news. On March 31, 1980, Jesse Owens died at a hospital in Tucson, Arizona, at the age of 66.

Immediately, plans were made to memorialize the great champion. Two thousand people attended his funeral at Oak Woods Cemetery in Chicago; Ohio

Owens finally received a college degree in 1972, when he was awarded an honorary doctor of athletic arts degree from Ohio State. He received many other accolades in the following years, including the Theodore Roosevelt Award (the National Collegiate Athletic Association's highest honor), the presidential Medal of Freedom, and induction into the Track and Field Hall of Fame.

State University announced that a new track complex would bear his name; athletic awards, scholarships, and annual track meets were created in his honor; and monuments were built to him in his childhood hometowns of Oakville, Alabama, and Cleveland, Ohio. Perhaps the greatest of these memorials was the one in Berlin, Germany. Jesse Owens Strasse became the new name of the street leading to the Olympic Stadium there.

In an effort to make sense of his life, Owens had written in *I Have Changed*: "The lives of most men are patchwork quilts. Or at best one matching outfit with a closet and laundry bag full of incongruous

Owens's granddaughter Gina Hemphill carries the Olympic torch around the Los Angeles Coliseum during the opening ceremonies of the 1984 Olympic Games.

accumulations." Astonishing athlete, advertising man, government emissary—Owens had worn these and many other hats, often at the same time, during his career. Perhaps it was his loss that he never found work that could compare with the athletic challenges of his amateur days, but in the patchwork quilt that he made of his life he touched millions of people in a way that he never could have by following a single line of work.

Owens always knew, however, that his greatest moment had been at the Berlin Olympics in 1936. That was when he proved himself more than a record-breaking athlete; the world discovered that he was a great sportsman as well. His showdown with Nazi chancellor Adolf Hitler has grown into a sports legend, but another aspect of the Games is even more significant. Owens's friendly competition with the German long jumper Luz Long will forever symbolize the way so-called enemies can work together to discover the best within themselves.

Thanks to the adoring attention of filmmaker Leni Riefenstahl's film *Olympiad*, it will always be possible to share the remarkable electric charge that went through the crowd in Berlin's Olympic Stadium in 1936. On the screen, an athlete like no other bursts from the starting line, instantly unfolding into an effortless, fluid stride. His feet seem to barely touch the ground. Before our eyes, he sails past all competitors and into the record books. The race, as Jesse Owens himself said, seems to be over in no time at all and to last an eternity. ❧

Owens's Olympic victories being immortalized in stone at the end of the 1936 Games.

CHRONOLOGY

——— ❦ ———

1913	Born James Cleveland Owens on September 12 in Oakville, Alabama
ca. 1922	Moves to Cleveland, Ohio
1927	Enrolls at Fairmount Junior High School; meets Coach Charles Riley
1930	Enrolls at East Technical High School
1933	Equals the world record in the 100-yard dash and breaks the world record in the 220-yard dash at the National Interscholastic Meet; enrolls at Ohio State University
1935	Breaks five world records and equals a sixth at the Big Ten Championships; marries Minnie Ruth Solomon
1936	Breaks the world record in the 100-yard dash; earns a berth on the U.S. Olympic team; wins Olympic gold medals in the 100 meters, 200 meters, long jump, and 400-meter relay; signs agency contract; loses amateur status
1937	Becomes a bandleader and the owner of a basketball team, softball team, and dry-cleaning company
1940	Resumes studies at Ohio State University
1941	Placed in charge of the Civilian Defense Office's national physical fitness program; takes a personnel job with Ford Motor Company
1945	Launches a public relations company
1950	Named the greatest track-and-field athlete in history by the Associated Press; appointed head of Illinois's Athletic Commission and Youth Commission; begins to travel widely as goodwill ambassador for the State Department
1965	Serves as running coach for the New York Mets
1970	Publishes *Blackthink: My Life as Black Man and White Man* and *The Jesse Owens Story*; awarded an honorary doctor of athletic arts degree from Ohio State University
1972	Publishes *I Have Changed*
1980	Dies of lung cancer on March 31 in Tucson, Arizona

FURTHER READING

Ashe, Arthur. *A Hard Road to Glory.* New York: Amistad-Warner, 1988.

Baker, William J. *Jesse Owens: An American Life.* New York: Free Press, 1986.

Cromwell, Dean B. *Championship Technique in Track and Field: A Book for Athletes, Coaches, and Spectators.* New York: McGraw-Hill, 1941.

Edwards, Harry. *The Revolt of the Black Athlete.* New York: Free Press, 1969.

Hart-Davis, Duff. *Hitler's Games.* New York: Harper & Row, 1986.

Johnson, William O., Jr. *All That Glitters Is Not Gold: The Olympic Games.* New York: Putnam, 1972.

Kusmer, Kenneth L. *A Ghetto Takes Shape: Black Cleveland.* Urbana: University of Illinois Press, 1976.

Mandell, Richard D. *The Nazi Olympics.* New York: Macmillan, 1971.

Owens, Jesse. *Blackthink: My Life as Black Man and White Man.* New York: William Morrow, 1970.

———. *I Have Changed.* New York: Morrow, 1972.

———. *Jesse: A Spiritual Autobiography.* Plainfield, NJ: Logos International, 1978.

———. *The Jesse Owens Story.* New York: Putnam, 1970.

Robertson, Lawson. *Modern Athletics.* New York: Scribners, 1932.

Wallechinsky, David. *The Complete Book of the Olympics.* New York: Viking Press, 1984.

INDEX

PICTURE CREDITS

TONY GENTRY holds an honors degree in history and literature from Harvard College. Formerly an award-winning news and feature editor at WWL Newsradio in New Orleans, he now works in New York City, where he is an avid runner and hopeful marathoner. His poetry and short stories have been published in *Turnstile* and *Downtown*. He is also the author of *Paul Laurence Dunbar* in the Chelsea House BLACK AMERICANS OF ACHIEVEMENT series.

NATHAN IRVIN HUGGINS is W.E.B. Du Bois Professor of History and Director of the W.E.B. Du Bois Institute for Afro-American Research at Harvard University. He previously taught at Columbia University. Professor Huggins is the author of numerous books, including *Black Odyssey: The Afro-American Ordeal in Slavery*, *The Harlem Renaissance*, and *Slave and Citizen: The Life of Frederick Douglass*.